CALL ME ANANIAS

RESTORING BROKEN LEADERS AND
EMPOWERING THOSE WHO ARE
CALLED TO HEAL THEM

AARON J. MOBLEY, JR.

DEDICATION

"Call Me Ananias," is dedicated to every individual that has had to carry the call of God during broken seasons. What strength it took you? What endurance you displayed? Even while you experienced circumstances that almost caused you to quit. This book is dedicated to your strength and the ability that is still within you to impact the lives of people all over the world for generations to come.

TABLE OF CONTENTS

INTRODUCTION

When perusing the countless accounts of men and women in the Bible, there is one individual that profoundly stands out. In my opinion, this account has been mostly overlooked. However, it holds powerful lessons that provide us with a roadmap that is without a doubt clear and that leads us back to the heart of Christ. This account is that of a man by the name of Ananias.

Let's not confuse him with the Ananias, who was married to a woman named Saphira. This Ananias was to be used to thrust the Apostle Paul into an assignment that is still touching people's lives all over the world. Have you ever heard of him? If you have, it may have just been in passing, as you continued to more significant moments in the life and ministry of the Apostle Paul. However, isn't this a mirror of how so many of God's most essential vessels are seen? Sometimes, they are not seen in the full power of their calling but as mere conduits and bridges that assist others in becoming who God has made them.

Have you ever thought of yourself as being the channel of blessing or the mode of transportation that individuals use to get from one place to another? Sometimes, we honestly don't see ourselves with that level of significance. Or, if we do, we might feel as though we are being used and not valued. If the truth is told, many of us think that our efforts aren't esteemed to the degree that they should.

Friends, there is nothing more honorable than to be used as a vessel of God in developing the life of another individual. Through that ministry, you can see firsthand what the power of God can do in restoring and healing others. Sadly, even after you have healed others, sometimes, you need healing yourself. This is why I have written this book.

I wholeheartedly believe that God's assignment on the earth is to heal. God is so passionate about healing that He sent his Son. According to Acts 10:38, Jesus was anointed by the Holy Ghost and went about doing good and healing all that were oppressed by the devil, for God was with Him. See, the mission of the Lord is to heal, and that includes leaders. Wow! Isn't that a novel idea? The idea that God wants to heal leaders as much as He does others who aren't leading.

Often, as individuals are being blessed, encouraged, and uplifted, we forget about those on the ministry's frontline. We neglect to see their suffering, hardships, disappointments, failures, and even the cracks in the vessels holding such powerful oil. Prayerfully, through this book, you will rediscover God's desire to heal the heart of leaders who are broken through people like Ananias and empower those who are the Ananias' in their generation.

Many of you reading this have been the bridge that was strong enough for others to cross and the connecting point that some needed to find God, healing, and restoration. Nevertheless, you have not felt appreciated for what you have done once those individuals made it safely to the other side. As a result, there is an opportunity for that brokenness to burrow in your heart. This is especially true when it is perpetuated because of the lack of gratefulness we receive when honestly giving our heart to others when theirs was almost gone.

Friends, if that hurt isn't managed well, it can develop into resentment that will hinder us from ministering to others and restoring those who have honestly been left behind. I want to ask you a question. How is your heart? How strong is it today in comparison to when you first started? By now, you probably have many scars from the battle. A few of those scars can be seen, but most of them are reserved for only the eyes of God. Those hidden wounds touch the heart of God and trigger His response in sending you individuals that can pour in that most precious oil and wine.

Beloved, it's not the time for you to quit or abandon your assignment on the earth. God wants you to finish it and produce all that He has created you to be in joy. If you would have an interview with leaders around you, you will find that not many walk out their leadership journey in joy. Many feel as though it's a burdensome assignment that has many woes but not much happiness. This idea is not the ideal plan of God for your soul. God desires that you bear the burden of what He has called you to do healthy, prosperous, but most of all, whole.

See, wholeness is one of the elements that we have left on the shelf as leaders. We have looked at ourselves as the bridges but haven't recognized the importance of maintenance. Maintenance is keeping up what has been erected and the inspection of cracks and defaults within the structure of that bridge. Sometimes, we carry the burden of many things, but not in the full strength that God has available. Inspecting your heart will show you where you are strong and identify the areas where you have become weak.

How many times have you said that you would never help another person? Or have been drained after assisting others in surviving, only to feel left behind when they did? If you are saying yes, to those questions, you are not alone.

If you are reading this book, you have probably experienced moments where your best intentions and efforts were briefly appreciated, but something was still missing. Yes, take that moment in because it is an area of the soul that longs to be filled. We just don't know how.

I want you to hear me when I say this as much as Paul needed Ananias; Ananias needed Paul. He had bravely stood for the cause of Christ, and because of this, he would now be asked to do something that most likely no one would have. Friends, your love for the heart of Christ will undoubtedly place you in precarious positions. You'll have to choose whether or not to just go with the popular opinions of the day. Do you know we have them, right? Sometimes, the consensus of the day chooses who deserves restoration and who doesn't, or who should be healed and who doesn't. But, when you are following the example of Christ, there is only one answer. Everyone deserves restoration and healing. That includes you. You are an Ananias, and you need an Ananias too!

Even after you have helped countless individuals manage some of the worst seasons of their lives, there must be a recovery that can only come from those you have helped the most. Unfortunately, many of the people you have served will never serve you in the same capacity. Why? Because people rarely see the need to minister to those who are called to be Ananias. The pains and disappointments of the Ananias' of the world aren't openly seen. They have learned to deal with them in private so that they can be strong for others. They behave in a way that is excellent and fortified because if they are seen breaking, they might lose the confidence of those who need their strength and courage.

What is interesting about this type of individual is that they are honestly not trying to pretend. Being strong is who God has graced them to be. They know that it is God who attracts brokenness to them, even as He pulls them towards the greatness that God has called them individually to be. However, in understanding this, we must note that some of the most resilient, battle-ready soldiers not only deal with the trauma of their battles but also the trauma of standing in wars that were never their own.

I cannot recall accurately the number of times, I have placed myself at the mercy of public opinion just so that I could stand for a friend in need, a leader who was at their wit's end, or even sometimes a stranger that everyone had given up on. I often knew the error and harm they had caused on themselves and others, but I refused to let them bleed to death, as others used the moment to destroy what

I knew God wanted alive. There were plenty of times I could've just kept my mouth shut, not answered calls, or just refused to pray, but I just could not remain silent. I had to stand up, be with them, whether in person or just in prayer.

In my own opinion, I am not a superman without feelings or emotions. In my thinking, I am mostly Clark Kent with a side of superman now and again. But to some, I am the strength that they didn't know they had, and for seasons at a time, I offer that to them to use as a lifeline as life's journey attempts to drown them in despair. Just call me Ananias.

Before the Apostle Paul was ever acknowledged as one of the scripture's most profound teachers, we find this man called Ananias. What's notable about his participation in the life of Paul is that he is only mentioned for a short period. Still, the effects of his touch would reverberate throughout the ministry of the Apostle Paul and would enable him to continue on the path and mission set before him.

Often, I think about those unsung heroes in our own lives.

When speaking about unsung heroes, I am talking about those individuals that God has called to take on some of the most controversial tasks and, often, a role that places them in harm's way. What's important about this is that this potential harm is not because of their actions but because of those they are called to support and heal.

Have you ever considered the unnecessary warfare that some of your greatest supporters experience because they are called alongside you? They don't necessarily see their role as dangerous, but they feel an overwhelming commitment to a purpose that we often don't see in ourselves. Often, the act of their love towards you blinds them from ever seeing that their stand with you might place them in the line of fire. Unfortunately, this is a common occurrence when standing in the gap and between life and death.

My purpose in writing this book is to honor those called to restore, heal and mend the lives and purposes of some of God's greatest servants. My assignment is to demonstrate the power of one person's decision in your life to rescue you from the bloodshed that almost destroyed everything that you were called to be. Lastly, it is to empower you to be that person in the life of another individual regardless of their public or private disappointments. You, too, can be an Ananias, the catalyst to an impact that will resound all over the world.

1

BRIDGES TO THE BROKEN

The powerful example that we have as believers is that our life is the most detailed roadmap an individual can have to discover Christ. Isn't that the ultimate goal of not only the scriptures but also the lives that are dedicated to its truth? In this age of significant technological advancement and social media prowess, there is still a method that God uses today that will outweigh every other tool man can create. That method is the changed life of someone that has come in contact with Christ.

What a fantastic idea this is? The idea that my interaction with one man could impact me and the way I perceive, handle, and understand everything and everyone around me. When was the last time that you considered your life, behavior, and interactions with anyone as being a direct reflection of how you channel the heart of Christ on the earth? Often, we don't take the time to do this, and as a result, we are demonstrating our flesh with only small pieces of the man Christ Jesus and the one we declare is the Lord and Savior of our lives.

If you are to get any of the truths that will come later in this book, you will have to make this the foundation of your learning. This foundation is that I handle the broken must be how Jesus Christ himself mirrored it on the earth.

I know that this might go against what you have learned from other influential individuals and the principles they've given. Still, our primary example to the hurting, failed, disappointed, and broken should be first through the lens of how Jesus Christ would have seen them. I know that the discernment of Christ saw and went well beyond what His public words were to certain people, but what He chose to display gives us a roadmap to how we should deal with the many failures and heartaches of our brothers and sisters.

If you allow me, I want to set a clear idea of how Jesus himself dealt with broken people. Before I continue, you should realize that we might be broken right now in some aspect of our lives. Sometimes, it displays as ministry fatigue, resentment, regret, the disappointments of failed ventures, or the grief over the loss of people that are no longer here, or those who are still here and for some reason aren't in our lives anymore. We all have been broken. You might be broken now.

I remember not too long ago; I received a word of prophecy from someone. As I listened attentively to the prophecy, it was like someone was unfolding recent events and how I had taken specific steps resulting from them. Now here's the kicker, he also began to point out experiences I had that brought me there. Those experiences weren't pleasant ones, though. They were hard lessons that I learned while leading people and the hurt I had experienced when I discovered that some people weren't as dedicated to my journey in God as I had demonstrated towards them.

I had been leading and continuing my journey in ministry, not recognizing that I was heartbroken. See, you would have to be a tenacious individual for you to understand what I am saying. You are stubborn to the point of no return. Despite every experience, you go on as if it never occurred. You're not willing to let your pain be presented in a way that makes you seem weak or not as confident as you should. I am that type of person, and I know that many of you are as well.

The mistake in that type of personality is that you are so intentional about moving forward that you don't appropriately give yourself the grace, space, and time to feel the emotions that the event has brought to the surface. Guess what? A wound that is covered but not healed has the opportunity to decay and rot. What has occurred recently for many of us is that we kept going but never got restored. There are a few reasons that I could note right now for why you weren't restored, but we'll talk about that later on.

Can you imagine my surprise and awe? For once, I realized that with as much Word as I knew, as much as I had a relationship with God, using my best attempts to continue the way I knew how, I realized that I was heartbroken and needed restoration. I needed to find individuals who would deal with me, not according to my accomplishments or their desire for me to maintain a platform. I needed to surround myself with individuals who would deal with me, as Christ did for so many others in the Bible. I needed to find individuals who would be the bridge to where I was and where I was going.

It's amazing how people forget that you are a human being just because of the title before your name. Instead of being concerned about your well-being during times of brokenness, they are more concerned with the extras that come with who you are. These are those who are more concerned with your church, ministry, business, finances, and connections than they are for the survival of your soul and heart.

This might be confusing for many of you because you think those things make up who you are. In your eyes, if those things aren't glamorized, then you are not as healthy as you need to be. This cannot be further from the truth. Many individuals have worked hard to maintain all of those things successfully, but it has been at the expense of the life that matters the most—their own.

FIGHTING TO SURVIVE

Several years ago, as I was fighting through one of the most challenging seasons of my life. I dealt with a scenario just like this. I don't have to identify this person, but it was someone that I trusted with my entire life. Unfortunately, I would later find out that he couldn't restore me and bring me into a place of health. I was looking for him to affirm that what I was doing for God would make sense in the light of what I was experiencing.

I remember contemplating sharing the deep depression I was in. It was the darkest cave I had ever seen and most certainly an unfamiliar place. I knew that it appeared as though I had everything together on the outside, but I also knew that there was an area of warfare that not many people realized was even occurring. How many of you are dealing with a silent battle right now? This battle is loud, boisterous, and fearful, but you feel as though you can't tell everyone its horrors because of who you are. This person knew the details, pain, and process of it all. Even with all of this knowledge, he still didn't have the wherewithal to help me the way I needed. Please understand, my sharing of these events is not to shame or place fault. It is to show you that many times, just because individuals have been present for you in one way, it doesn't mean that they will have the grace to help you in other.

As the events go on, I do decide to share the heart of my experience with him. I can vividly recall saying to him, "I feel like I'm about to lose it," "I think I need medication," "Do you think that I'll live beyond this," "I think I need to take a break from ministry and focus on getting better and healed."

To me, I was as clear as I could have ever been, but to my amazement, the response wasn't what I had expected at all. As I listened, I didn't hear answers that signified that I had been heard. Yes, he listened, but I wasn't heard. The part of me that was screaming on the inside was muffled by his need for me to simply, "Preach through it." Beloved, this tore my heart to shreds because what was most important was the need for me to continue displaying ministry and growing a solid church instead of ensuring that I most of all stayed alive. This might not make sense to everyone reading this book, but I know that it tugs on the heartstrings of some of you that have been in similar situations with people you thought would understand your brokenness.

When God began dealing with Hannah's heart in 1 Samuel, we see that she was married but was still not producing. She had everything that the others had, and instead of her being able to give her husband a child, she was forced to watch others produce what she had longed to. When leading others or simply following Christ, you will encounter situations just like her. To the apparent eye, you should display more prosperity, be happier, or even more joyful, but something is missing. There's a void that only proper healing and restoration can fill.

The Bible says that her rival began to provoke her sorely. I believe that whatever Peninnah could have done to torment her, she did. But here's another aspect of that story. Despite what was being done to her, that was not the main focus of her bitterness. Her bitterness was coming from within her. She knew what she wanted. She realized what she should be giving her husband, but something within her was still broken. It was her understanding of herself and her pain that brought her in front of Eli the Priest.

However, instead of recognizing the internal distress, he diagnosed her outward display as something opposite from what was going on. When is the last time that you made decisions, and instead of others seeing beyond it, they began to categorize it as something else? They attributed your pain to something that you could change outwardly and failed to support the work that needed to happen inside. My goal in writing this book is that you will begin understanding that the majority of the construction that needs to take place in your life is internal. There are hidden places that you rarely visit within that are still occupied by situations that you refuse to confront.

One of the most courageous exploits you will ever be able to do for God is the journey of systematically uncovering the woes of your journey. It's very common to spiritualize everything, but all of us arrive at a point where we realize that we need help, and even though we have God, we need someone else too. I know this is a bitter pill for many of us to swallow because we have not fully leaned into the idea of walking alongside individuals transparently. Still, I hope that by the end of this book, you will see its significance to you and the survival of your purpose. In light of that, I want you to realize that when God assigns support to you, their stand with you will be in the full light of everything that you are, everywhere you have been, and even the inner workings of your mind, will and emotions. Nothing will catch them off-guard. Their assignment with you is a grace that has been given to them by God, and when God dispatches individuals, they have the strength to bear it all. When is the last time that you have submitted to an Ananias and exposed it all? When's the last time you were able to tell the gritty emotions that plague your heart at night? Or the sudden bouts with depression that attempt to torture your soul directly after a powerful church service? If you're a leader reading this book, I'm sure that you can identify being used of God extensively in the service of others but not feeling as if anyone was concerned about you.

See, the mere act of preaching is a sedative to the natural

emotions that still have to be dealt with. While you are ministering, you are probably feeling invincible. The crowd is clapping and, on their feet, making you feel like a superstar, but when the robe and collar come off, you still have to deal with not only your emotions but the unwise decisions that may have possibly thrown your life into a tailspin. Yes, let's talk about it all. Brokenness has no barriers. It extends itself through every stage of our life and can be the wall to us ever really seeing the success we need in our soul first and then in our outer world.

Hannah was in bitterness of soul, and no one around her could give her what she needed. Her husband tried the best way he knew how to satisfy her. The Bible says that he gave her a more worthy portion of meat. He thought that if I did this, it would silence the cries she was experiencing. Here's the thing. I want you to release everyone in your life from their possible inability to give you what you need. Those individuals that tried in the past but failed simply didn't have it to give. The truth is that some weren't assigned to provide it.

Some of our most trusted leaders and confidants weren't taught how to be lasting support emotionally and mentally to anyone, especially if they don't know how to be it to themselves. Many of them have never really stood in the face of their heartbreaks and definitely don't have the resource to help mend yours. Learning to release those who don't have the ability to heal is the doorway to receiving those that can.

One way that I have learned to remain honorable to every individual in my life is to value the resource they are designed to bring. I don't look for them to provide what I know they don't currently have. I want you to think about the wise men who brought gifts to Jesus. They all carried something different with a purpose attached. When you begin to expect everyone to provide the same thing, you are dishonoring each individual's role in your life.

In addition to that idea, has anyone ever been mad with you for not giving them something? But what they didn't realize is that you didn't have it to give or couldn't afford to give it away? The same thing happens in relationships when we don't discern who we are connected to healthily. People shouldn't have to overperform to stay connected to you or act like they have more than they do. Be careful of expecting support in areas where others are still falling. It's a recipe for disasters and the introduction of an ended relationship.

Often, when a crisis hits our lives, we expect people to know what to do, but often, they don't have the grace or the assignment to restore you in the nature that would advance God's purpose for your life. You'll be going through an emotional season, and they'll invite you to preach? Or, you can be mentally exhausted, and they'll ask you to help out with a conference. None of those things actually help heal what is ailing you. However, I have learned that people do what was done to them, whether it was helpful or not. They reproduce help in the way that they received help. So, when your outlook on support is wrong, you'll wrongfully support those around you in the same way. Wow! Lord, forgive us for helping people in a way that wasn't helpful but hurtful.

Think about this scenario. One of your friends is moving and needs a truck to help transport some heavy furniture. You offer your vehicle to them to use to get the job done. They send you the address and patiently wait for your arrival. Hours pass, and no truck arrives. They call you to see where you are, and you discover that you have been sitting with an empty truck at the wrong address. This is what happens when people think they are helping you unload. The only thing they are doing is adding more frustration and baggage onto an already heavy load. Learn to listen attentively to the brokenness of those around you. Ask specific questions about how you can support them, but don't just take their initial answer. Listen deeply to hear by the Spirit of God what they are not saying, and using the wisdom of God, support them in the areas that they might not be ready to speak. One of the hidden qualities about this type of Ananias is that you don't have to say everything to do everything. Let that sink in while we continue.

See, what Hannah needed was not just to be happy. She wanted a child. Out of all of her labor and faithfulness, there was still something that she needed from God. As much as you want to blame others, I want you to understand that God must orchestrate this next level of restoration in your life. Also, you must yield to those that He sends. We sometimes miss out on our seasons of repair because our help doesn't look like who we expect.

Often, you're waiting on those you have been there for the most, to be the ones who restore and bring health back to you. Unfortunately, this is not the way it happens most of the time. In my experience, God will sometimes send people who don't align with anything that you have known to be the channel of healing that you need during some of your most desperate times.

"Do not neglect to extend hospitality to strangers [especially among the family of believers—being friendly, cordial, and gracious, sharing the comforts of your home and doing your part generously], for by this some have entertained angels without knowing it."

Hebrews 13:2 Amplified

When God determined to remind Abraham and Sarah concerning His promise to them, he sends them three angels fashioned as men. In Genesis 18, we observe as Abraham is sitting in the doorway of his tent. Suddenly he sees three men approaching him. Without hesitation, he invites them to sit down and have a meal.

How many of us would have been that cordial to strangers just passing by? No, some of us would have gone into our tents and acted like we didn't see them. However, I think that there was something significant going on in the heart of Abraham. I believe that he was expecting someone. Who? He probably didn't know, but someone. He had known since hearing the voice of God at first that God wanted to give him a son and generations after that, but he had not seen it happen. In his heart, he was expecting some sort of confirmation to what he knew God wanted.

See, before your Ananias can ever arrive in your life, you must keep your expectation of restoration alive and be open to receiving from those individuals when they appear. I want you to get rid of all of your preconceived notions of how and through who God will bring your deliverance. As long as you've got your standards, you forfeit God's ability to use those that have His heart and are qualified the most.

As the meal concludes, one of the men asks Abraham, "Where is your wife?" Of course, like any good wife, she had listened to the conversation all along. You must remember that she had taken this step of faith right along with him and was patiently waiting on the Prophecy as well. Unfortunately, her outlook had become dim, and her expectation was not as strong as his.

The man, who we know now as an angel, begins to declare again that Sarah would have a son. She immediately laughs. It's hard to tell what the complete source of this laughter stemmed from. Possibly, she doubted God's ability to make it happen, but she could've also not trusted the source of this news. Sometimes, in our effort to discern and be spiritual, we have become blind to how God will occasionally use foolish things and those who appear ridiculous to give us the restorative Word we need. Listen, if you have read the Bible, you see that God will use anything and anyone to bring the healing you need. Just think about that dirty raven that God used to sustain Elijah as he was waiting at the Brook Cherith or that donkey that God used to save the life of the Prophet Balaam as he was on his way to curse God's chosen people. Don't discount those that God sends in your life in this season. He has an intention behind their arrival and will use their obedience as a tool of healing to advance his purpose in your life.

RESTORATION DOESN'T HAVE TO COME FROM WHO YOU EXPECT!

Let's be honest. I believe that some of your most

encouraging seasons have been through individuals who you least expected, but some of your most hurtful times have been at the hands of familiar people that you looked to the most.

While Abraham is cordial to them and listens as they declare the fruit that would come from Sarah's womb, the Bible says that Sarah sat in the tent and laughed. She possibly could not believe that these strangers could declare what she knew she wanted the most. In addition, she could have doubted that she had the ability within herself to produce what she had always longed for.

Hear this! Whenever God sends your Ananias to you, that individual will spark the hope of your past. They will remind you of God's promise to you and the restoration that has always been his plan. What would be most important in this illustration is how Abraham received his help. Yes! That's the same question that I would like to ask you. How will you receive the support that God is about to send to you? Possibly, that person is already present, but you are not receiving them in a manner that is honorable to their role and contribution in your life.

HUMILITY AND HOSPITALITY:
THE DOORWAY TO RESTORATION

Let's remember the Shunammite woman in 1 Kings 4:8. The Bible says that one day this woman notices Elisha and urges him to eat. The first part of accepting the invitation to healing is humility and hospitality. Humility demonstrates your ability to reject pride or arrogance as a lifestyle. See, many people are humble only in certain situations, but humility must be a way of life that is common for you when you are expecting God daily. God resists the proud and gives grace to the humble.

The second facet of that is that because of her humility; she was given to hospitality. She was open to serving others through the resources that she had. Often, when you are on the path to restoration, God will provide ways for you to demonstrate on the earth hospitality to someone in need. God wants to see if you are willing to give someone what you know you need as well, even if it's different. Elisha needed something, but so did she.

Every time Elisha passed by this woman would make sure that he was fed. One day, revelation comes on her through her consistent lifestyle of humility and hospitality. She sees something in him that she probably didn't see before. She notices now that he is a Holy Man of God. Often, God will hide your gift in open sight, waiting and watching how you handle it before you even know that it's for you. In response to what she is now seeing in him, she was currently responsible for elevating the way she handled him.

Before, she was just led to give him food, but she had to elevate her submission to his role in her life because of the current way she was now viewing him. She now realizes that this man wasn't just passing by. He was sent to her, and she had to make him feel welcome. Sometimes, when God sends restoration to us, we shun it and those that God works through. We don't make ourselves as available as we should. We treat them as average or with less honor as some of the more notable voices around us. I want you to begin to think about those that God allowed to pass by you in your past seasons. How did you handle them? Did you use their names and voices as a platform? Or did you realize that God had sent them for something far greater. He sent them to save your life.

This revelatory woman goes to her husband and urges him to make room for the man of God. Can you believe this? Her insight into this man's role in her life constrains her to make more space for his ministry in their home. They go over and beyond to make his voice feel comfortable and available. Many times, we have not received healing ministry because we didn't make those voices feel comfortable. We made them feel like nuisances and unwanted guests. This couple would not make that mistake.

Because of their humility and hospitality, the Prophet Elisha is led to find out what she needed. Her response is like what many of us would give, even though we knew we needed something more. She says that she needs nothing, but God knew better than that. Elisha sends the servant back with a prophetic word concerning a son that she would have. This son would give her what she had wanted without ever having to say it.

Friends, God intends to give you what you can't adequately express. There are silent petitions, areas of brokenness, and unprocessed pain that God is violently going to confront in your life. Will you be open to it? Will you wholeheartedly receive who He sends? Will you say yes to the recovery you know you need? Hopefully, every answer was a resounding, yes. If so, get ready. Your Ananias is coming!

2

DENS, CAVES, AND STRONGHOLDS: SOMEONE IS COMING FOR YOU

Most likely, you have been the individual who has always run into the crisis of others. You've probably been the constant source of encouragement and support to everyone in your family, your friends, and even the congregations you might lead. You may also be the person that feels forgotten. I believe we all have felt that way at one time or another.

In the process of serving God and doing what we feel will please him, sometimes we arrive at points that just don't make sense. To have so many powerful visions and revelations and then to be placed in some of the darkest pits doesn't add up to all that you have invested in others and the kingdom of God. It's easy to recognize brokenness when it comes from other individuals, but how do we reconcile brokenness when we feel like it is coming from God? Countless leaders worldwide are in this mental and spiritual dilemma, the place of believing in God with all of your heart while serving him in such disappointment because of the pains He has allowed you to endure. I know how that feels. I have been there a time or two myself. Waiting for someone to help you make sense of what you're experiencing, but the wait seems as if it will never end. You feel forgotten.

Yes, I know that God never forgets us and that He keeps impeccable records of our service to Him. However, what is crucial in the healing process is to acknowledge any area that we do. God isn't upset at you disclosing your feelings and your need for Him to show you the same power; He has used you to demonstrate. If you're reading this, you have probably been used by God to do some extraordinary things. You've most likely laid hands on the sick and seen them recover. You've probably ministered to the deepest depressed person, and God lifted them, but little did they know that you were in a darker cave than they were.

Isn't this remarkable? That even on our best days of being a vessel of God's power, we can be in the lowest place in our hearts. Beloved, you are not alone in this experience. Some of God's greatest vessels have felt forgotten too. I want to ask you a question that I pray will expose any area in your heart that might feel this way. That question is, "Have you received as much from God as you have expected?" I know that we are taught to be grateful and appreciative for our daily bread, but what do you do when you feel as though you have invested more than you have reaped? You've been diligent to sow well into the lives of those you lead and to guide them through the heart of Christ. Yet, there are things in your soul that are still broken, and you have been left without an explanation.

The Prophet Elijah was also in this type of scenario in 1 Kings 18. Elijah had just overcome a significant challenge with the prophets of Baal. God had just shown them his power in an unexplainable way. However, after this, Elijah is put on the run by Jezebel's threats and finds himself under a juniper tree, requesting that he die. He wasn't asking for rest. He was asking for death. Doesn't this seem drastic? To some of you, it is, but to others, you understand. The weight of the call to lead can feel overwhelming at times. The history of triumphs and disappointments can often plague the mind as we compare our sometimes-challenging experiences with the smooth ride of fame and glory that others display. I know that comparison kills, but you've got to admit that sometimes we've looked over at the lawn that was greener and imagined what it would feel like to live there for just a day or two. Have you ever experienced success, great church or ministry growth, increased revenue in business, and loving-supporting friends, but still felt like enough was enough? This is what was occurring in the heart of Elijah. He had been going and going. From one act of obedience to another, he was now on the run again. Enough was enough.

In my over 35 years of ministry and almost 17 years of

pastoring, I've discovered that sometimes we just want a season of rest. I'm not talking about a season of just being able to be lazy or sleep all the time. I'm speaking about a season that is automated and that we don't have to be on-guard, hands on the wheel constantly, and on ready 24 hours a day. We all long for a time where whatever resources we need just roll in like the wind, and the support we desire just showers on us like the April rains. However, sometimes, it appears like this season is never going to come. So, as a result, we just stop. We get bogged down emotionally and mentally and seemingly remain functional on the outside, but the wheels of innovation and motivation are spinning more slowly than they usually did. Elijah had gotten to this point.

People who aren't aware of the inner workings of a leader can think that you are ungrateful. They say, "You should be glad to be used of God," or "If I had your anointing, I'd be so grateful." Little do they know, the amount of responsibility all of that carries and the days when you would instead be anointed but not leading, especially if you feel like you are leading alone.

A leader can be surrounded by many people and still feel

this way. Sometimes, we can feel as though people just don't get it. They don't get why I'm doing what I'm doing or why it's important. A leader can also feel unloved for the person that they are to that body. See, a leader must feel love for the individual they are and not just for the things they do. Have you ever asked yourself this question? If I stopped doing what I'm doing, would they still love me? Would they still think I was a good leader? Or would they just simply walk away.

Very recently, I was in the middle of many of these questions. I had led a ministry for almost 17 years. Suddenly, right in the middle of the pandemic, I was faced with a question. Is it time? This wasn't the first time this question came around. Every year for over ten years, I had asked myself this same question, but I quickly answered no every time. However, 2020 was different. This time, I couldn't answer so abruptly. For seven days, I was plagued with thoughts and questions. I inquired of the Lord but also searched my heart. My mind went to the many families and lives that my one decision would affect. I knew what my mind was telling me, but my heart was giving me mixed signals.

I wondered whether they would fight for me as I had fought for them. I knew what I needed to do, but there was something in me that asked whether they would offer any resistance. No! I wasn't expecting a protest. Well, maybe a small one, LOL. Perhaps a few of the saints on my front lawn yelling, "Heaven No, we won't go!" would have sufficed. I wondered whether they would still love me as the Man of God that had led them valiantly these many years or if they would simply walk away and find a new spiritual home. All of these questions rolled around in my mind for seven whole days.

After that time of meditation, I began to reach out to those familiar with this season in my life. Many of the people close to me had heard me speak about this and were very aware of my contemplation. Even though they had understood before, this time, it was different. They heard me. They didn't just listen to my feelings and thoughts, but they listened to what my soul was saying, and I think they listened to what the season was calling me to do. Can I pause and ask you a question, "What about your friends?" Are you surrounded by individuals who have your best interest in mind, or are they just concerned with your status and prominence as a leader? Is your fame what fosters your connections? Or does your circle care more about your life than they do the ministry you lead. Now, don't get me wrong. I believe that every leader cares and loves the churches they shepherd like family, but your friends must see you just as valuable.

After hearing their hearts and submitting to the wisdom of God, I made my decision. I was sure, I was confident, but I was afraid. For almost half of my life, this was all that I had known. I had done many other things, but pastoring was the launching pad for all of those things. My life centered around the ministry and the people I led. Because I'm an introvert, these were the people that made me feel comfortable. What would their departure in this way mean to me emotionally? I leaped and announced my resignation. No one saw it coming. I had discussed it many times before in messages and sermons, but I don't believe that anyone foresaw the day coming.

To my disappointment, there was no protest. There weren't lines of cars suddenly appearing on my street with flowers and cards that said thank you. There weren't long letters written detailing all of the things that I had done not for the ministry but for them. I did receive a few responses, but nothing to the degree that I had slightly hoped for. See, when a leader makes transitions, one of the things that makes it smoother is the loving and public support they receive from those who were in the season their exiting. To know that it wasn't just about what you did, but about who you were.

But guess what? God wasn't going to allow me to transition alone. There was a group of people who refused to leave me. Where were we going? What was I going to do with them? I had no clue, but they insisted that they come along for the ride. For six months, I did nothing. I offered no teaching or ministry presentations. It was kind of like I was Moses and had gone up to the mount to talk with God, and they were sitting at the foot of the mountain waiting. I remember sharing with them that I had no idea what the next steps were, but if they still wanted me to lead them spiritually, that I would. This group embraced my next season and was so happy for me.

They began bringing gifts, financial resources, encouraging words, and listening ears as I poured my heart about what I felt the next seasons would bring.

Finally, I realized. These individuals didn't just love what I did for them. They loved me for me. I wasn't Elijah under the juniper tree anymore. I was the Elijah that would eat and travel in strength for many days to come.

As we continue to look at this story, it's easy to scoff at his weakness in light of what God had just done. For us to fully expose his depression, we must take a moment to dig deeper. Firstly, as he is confronting the prophets of Baal, he says something interesting. He says that he is the only one left *(1 Kings 18:22)*. He mentions that the number of the prophets of Baal was 450 men. In the natural, the odds were certainly stacked against him.

Isn't that how we sometimes feel when we are doing our best to serve God and lead his people? How in the world would God place this much pressure on one person? Yes! You have a staff and a group of people supporting you, but it still feels as though you are standing alone sometimes when you are leading.

If we go further into the journey of Elijah, we'll see that leaving the juniper tree was only half of his deliverance. Isn't that powerful? Often, as leaders, we assume that one therapy session is enough or one good service will do the trick. However, freedom must be an intentional process and most certainly a consistent dialogue with God. Having the strength to go on wasn't the issue for Elijah. It was the remaining questions that plagued his heart. Even after leaving the tree, Elijah finds himself somewhere else. In 1 Kings 19, he comes to Horeb, the mount of God, and finds himself in a cave. It was there that God begins a conversation with him concerning his life and what was occurring. This dialogue would also shed light on what his legacy would look like and the support that was coming to help him.

Friends, don't be afraid to have a talk with God about where you are. He is ready to share with you some information that will secure your heart concerning the future. God asks him, "What are you doing here?" Of course, God knew why he was there, but God wanted him to say it. Sometimes, we are feeling things that don't match the reality of God's plans for our lives. The emotions of it all blind us that we don't see the future as being as bright as it is. After telling God how much he had done for Him and how lonely he was, God gives him the instructions that he needed. If you allow your heart to rule your next steps, you'll miss the greater plan that God has for your purpose and life. God reveals to Elijah that he wasn't alone at all. He had thousands left in Israel who had not submitted to Baal, and that He had even set aside someone to walk with him for the remainder of his journey.

When you have an honest talk with God, you open the channels of support you have been so desperate to receive. Often, we feel that the best help we could've ever received is lost in an old season that's expired. But this is not so. God still has a reserved people. Someone is coming for you!

DENS, CAVES, AND STRONGHOLDS

I remember vividly asking God to bring a clear understanding to something occurring in my life. I knew why it had happened, but I didn't know why God had allowed it to happen. Hopefully, that makes complete sense to you. There are always external reasons why certain things occur, but when we have been taught concerning God's supernatural power to stand in between earthly events, and it doesn't happen, our hearts begin to wander. We begin to ask ourselves questions like, "God, you could have stopped that," "I know I was wrong, but where was the grace you showed others?" "What did allowing that to happen achieve, and how did that bring you glory?"

Friends, it's okay to ask God the hard questions. When I think about these types of questions, I remember the question that Gideon asked the Lord in Judges 6. To understand the severity of his question, you must understand what was occurring at that time. The Bible says that the children of Israel were behaving wickedly in the sight of the Lord. As a consequence, God delivers them into the hands of the Midianites. To hide, they made dens, caves, and strongholds in the mountains.

Remember those three things: dens, caves, and strongholds. A den is a small hollow place, usually on the side of a hill or among rocks. It's usually used by wild animals for shelter or concealment as not to be seen. A cave is a large, naturally occurring cavity formed underground or in the face of a cliff or hillside. If you look at the words as verbs, the difference is that a den is to hide oneself, and to cave is to surrender.

Wow! How many seasons have you been hiding? Making small cutouts in your life where you can conceal who you are? See, for many of you, the power of who you are isn't hidden by anyone else. You are hiding. You feel as if you do; the warfare that you're experiencing will cease. It's kind of like you are giving the giant an excuse as to why you are no longer a threat.

Some of you are choosing to live in dens so that you can just blend in. You no longer want the stage or the popularity. You've seen the retaliation that comes from those who are on the frontline, and you no longer want to be a part of it. You'd rather be in the background serving God than ever to have to go through what you have. Beloved friends, please hear this. You cannot hide when God has made you great. I don't care if you run to the farthest extent of the globe. Someone in that place will see exactly who you are. The den is not your home.

In addition, some of us live in caves. We have caved under the pressure of being the leader that everyone looks to. We no longer put up a fight when adversity comes.

We give in and just simply accept every loss as being the will of God. We have chosen to live in a cave that not many people know we do. But friends, someone is coming for you.

Do you remember David? After being anointed by God as the next King, David begins to be threatened and taunted by Saul, whose heart had grown wicked. He is filled with jealousy and seeks to kill who God anointed. Whenever jealousy is rooted in the heart, murder is the next avenue to destroy the assignment God gives us. Saul was after David's assignment.

Whenever God has placed something in your hands to accomplish, you must know that there will be a target on your back to stop you from fulfilling it. I don't say that for you to become frightened. I share it so that you can begin understanding why certain things occur. Assignments always attract assassins. If you're going to continue leading, you'll have to become knowledgeable concerning what and who your assassins are. What might be an assassin to your purpose might not be one to mine. All of us must become intimately aware of what the enemy uses against us to distract us and the destiny ahead.

David is now on the run, and the Bible says in 1 Samuel 22 that he finds refuge in the Cave of Adullam. Here we go. Another leader in a caved situation. What's important to understand here is that David didn't do anything wrong. He was anointed by the choice of God while he was minding his own business. It was God that saw greater in him when he might've not seen anything of power within himself. He was okay with serving his father and doing things that would possibly bring him into favor. However, he didn't realize that the favor he sought from one father would come from a far greater father. God would begin to favor him among his brothers and the house that really never honored him.

Favor will cause people to fight against you. We see this scenario time and time again in the Word of God where people are set a part for the use of God, and because of that, the enemy becomes infuriated. Saul wanted to kill David. And, just as he wanted to kill David, the enemy wants to kill leaders who God anoints to heal and restore. See, if the masses are to be destroyed, the devil's plan is always first to assassinate those that lead them.

We can look through the annuals of any government or

people and track individuals who were on the brink of changing a generation. We'll see that those individuals constantly lived under the threat of retaliation and, in some cases, the danger of death. How many times have you allowed the enemy to threaten you? How many times did you go into your cave until the threat passed over? David found refuge in a cave called Adullam. What's powerful about that example is that even though he was in a cave. Someone came looking for him.

The word Adella can either mean to turn aside, to retreat or find refuge. During this course of history, it is important to note that David passed up several opportunities to kill Saul, even though Saul was attempting to kill him. See, sometimes, your frustration as a leader comes from God not allowing you to do to them as they have done to you. God still compels you to love, minister, encourage and support, while many times, they give you the exact opposite. Often, that will cause you to find a cave.

David refused to fight in a way that would not honor God. He had the chance to kill Saul while he was asleep but didn't. He realized that even as he was anointed, so was

Saul, and he dared not destroy God's anointed. Friends, I know it might not look like it now, but God will reward you for every time you didn't seek vengeance because of what was being done to you. The Bible states that because David honored God, soon he and those that met him in the cave were known throughout Israel for their deeds and great exploits.

Another interesting and empowering idea is that even though David was on the run and living in caves, God still had a remnant that saw him as he was. They could've cared less where he was. They knew who he was. I want to declare into your life today that someone is coming for you, and you won't have to fake anything. They're not concerned with what you have, the number of supporters applauding you, or the platform that is branding your name. They see you in a far greater way than you can ever imagine. Those three captains came and found him. I'm sure that their arrival stimulated something in David's heart that was probably growing dim. See, there's sometimes light in us that was once brilliant but became dim while living in a caved situation. However, when God sends reinforcement, it does not only help you to fight but also provides strength for you to live.

We often speak about the courageous stand of David, but have you ever considered the commitment of those three chief men who met him as he was hiding in that cave? Just like David, many of us have had to hide out. We were often wondering if those we had served the most would come and sit with us as we contemplated our next move.

It takes sharp vision into the purpose of a broken leader to stand in the face of their opposition and do what many refused to do. Not only did they meet him where he was, but they were also willing to continue the assignments he gave even though it placed them in grave danger. I want to show you here that many times the Ananias you seek is right in the midst of you. They are the ones who still show up despite the sounds of battle that they hear rallied against you. They see you as being worth the fight, worth the scars, and worth the danger. Don't forget about them when you come out of that cave.

There's one more thing that I want to show you about this particular cave. Many political commentators have used the term "Cave of Adella" to signify any small group remote from power but planning to return. Wow! So, the cave has no more power than you give it because while you are there, you still have the opportunity to plan your next move. Get ready to come out of that cave. Someone is coming for you!

Before we end this chapter, let's continue our talk from Judges 6. The Midianites had burned all of their substance. Everything that they had sowed was now gone. They had found in dens, caves, and strongholds, but now the Lord sends a prophet to them to remind them of His word, but He didn't stop there. After that, He sends an angel to a man by the name of Gideon. At this point, Gideon was hiding wheat from the Midianites. He wasn't doing anything that would make him stand out as a courageous leader. He wasn't sharpening his sword or shining his armor. He was hiding his substance from the enemy. To many, he would've seemed like a coward, but to God, he was much more. Guess what? You are much more.

It's easy for people to criticize the steps you've had to take or the decisions you have made, but I want you to understand that you were never alone. It was the hand of

God guiding your movements, and even when you felt uneasy, it was God who continued to balance you in every place that mattered. They may have called you a coward. God called you courageous. See, it takes courage to take the leaps and bounds that you have. It takes boldness to stand in the presence of many and declare what you have. Friends, you are not weak. You are strong.

"And the angel of the Lord appeared unto him, and said unto him, The Lord is with thee, thou mighty man of valor. And Gideon said unto him, Oh my Lord, if the Lord be with us, why then is all this befallen us? And where be all his miracles which our fathers told us of, saying, Did not the Lord bring us up from Egypt? but now the Lord hath forsaken us, and delivered us into the hands of the Midianites." **Judges 6:12-13 KJV**

When the Lord speaks to Gideon, he labels him very opposite than others would have. He calls him a mighty man of valor. Wow! He's hiding wheat, but he's valiant. Yes, God knew who Gideon was despite what he was doing. He knew that His plan for him was far greater than the opposition that was now coming against them.

Gideon's response was just like what some of ours would have been. He asked God about where the miracles were? He had heard the stories of how God had brought the children of Israel out of Egypt and the powerful signs He displayed. However, he wasn't seeing them. Leaders, this sounds like some of the questions in our hearts, doesn't it? God quickly counteracts Gideon's doubt and commands him to take on His might. He gives Gideon his marching orders and begins detailing what he would do and the great exploits that would be seen through his life. God sent someone to Gideon just like I feel this book is being sent to you.

Before we close this chapter, I want to point out to you two important things. When God begins to encourage their hearts here in Judges 6, He first sends a prophet. He sends a man. The second time He encourages them, He sends an angel. He starts naturally but then elevates the conversation as He sends an angel to Gideon. Here's my point. Those that God sends to you in this season of your life will be more spiritual than natural. They'll have spiritual discernment into who you are and what their assignment is in your life. You won't have to convince them or overly explain your past failures or disappointments. They've already heard from God and are clear about what role they are supposed to play in your life. Don't be afraid to receive them. Someone is coming for you!

One of the greatest examples of this can be found in Acts 16:9-10. It says, *"And a vision appeared to Paul in the night; There stood a man of Macedonia, and prayed him, saying, Come over into Macedonia, and help us. And after he had seen the vision, immediately we endeavored to go into Macedonia, assuredly gathering that the Lord had called us for to preach the gospel unto them."*

Isn't that powerful? Paul didn't get his directives by anything natural. No one came knocking on the door. He didn't receive counsel from men. He received his directions from God through this vision. In this vision, he knew exactly where he was to go and the assignment that would be there. So, when I prophetically declare that someone is coming, this is what I am speaking about. The next group of individuals that God sends to you will be spiritually supportive because of their relationship with God and His will concerning you.

There are other powerful examples of this. We could quickly talk about the wise men and shepherds sent to Jesus, demonstrating the honor God is about to send in your life. We could spend some time sharing about how God sent Phillip over to the Ethiopian Eunuch, who was reading the Prophet's book, and talk about how God will send people in your life to bring understanding. We could even take time and talk about Joseph and the many perils that he saw while walking out his coat of many colors and how God used one man to remember him, ushering him into prominence in Egypt.

My point in sharing all of those events is to confirm that someone is coming for you. It doesn't matter where you are right now in your leadership or support role journey. God has already dispatched someone to come and find you. They're not coming because of an advertisement. They are coming because they have heard God concerning you. Your name has been in their heart, and they won't rest until they fulfill God's assignment in being there for you as He has designed. Someone is coming for you!

3

RESTORATION AFTER REJECTION

One of the most painful experiences a leader can experience is that of rejection. If you have felt this on any level, you already know that sometimes it has lasting implications. It will affect the way you lead, the openness you share, and your ability to love those the Lord sends. If you have been a leader for any period, you most likely have been in this season before.

When God dispatches leaders into the vineyard, He does

with such passion and power. It's kind of like He places this armor on you that seems unbeatable. I'm reminded of this idea when he calls the Prophet Jeremiah. Even after Jeremiah's hesitation, God tells him to make his face like flint, a hard stone. He commands Jeremiah to stand in the face of all that oppose him and that He would be right there with him to deliver him.

What's important to note here is that God's commands did not eliminate Jeremiah's humanness. He was still a natural man occupying a supernatural assignment. When you don't accept this reality, the woes of life will overwhelm you and overtake you.

In this chapter, I want to talk about restoration after rejection. As I began writing, immediately, my mind rested on the narration of the Prophet Samuel and his relationship with King Saul in 1 Samuel 9-16. Israel had desired a king even though they had a well-abled prophet leading them. They wanted to be like the other nations. As a result, or as some of you may see it, as a consequence, God gives them what they wanted. He chooses a man by the name of Saul. There's something about these Saul's, huh? Yes. This Saul, too, was a character. He was a man of war but would be led by the guidance of the Prophet Samuel to become a different man.

After God identifies this new King, Samuel gives Saul some precise instructions. He tells him to go to the hill of God and find a group of prophets coming down from the high place. They would be in worship with tambourines, flutes, and harps, and that he was to get in the middle of them. As they begin to prophesy, the Bible says that he also prophesied with them and became another man.

See, much of the restoration that we need as leaders is prophetic. Sometimes, we run to natural sources to regain strength, but the truth is that if we are not being guided prophetically, we are lost. Saul is obedient to the instructions he received from the Prophet Samuel. The people who formerly knew him were baffled. They could not reconcile the new Saul they were seeing.

As the story unfolds, Saul becomes prideful and disobedient to the instructions of God through the Prophet Samuel. He becomes unhinged and defies the person's influence that God sent to him to guide and protect his rule. Sometimes, as leaders, we place ourselves in harm's way when we become too large for the voice of wisdom in our lives. Everyone needs a Samuel, just like David would need a Nathan. Maybe we'll talk about that later on, but for now, let's continue sharing.

Consequently, God decides to rip the kingdom from Saul's hands and throw into motion, His plan to anoint and prepare another king. Have you ever thought about the rejection that was occurring in the heart of Saul at the beginning of this entire story? If you haven't, let me remind you of what the Lord said to him as Israel demanded a king.

"And the Lord said unto Samuel, Hearken unto the voice of the people in all that they say unto thee: for they have not rejected thee, but they have rejected me, that I should not reign over them."

1 Samuel 8:7 KJV

See, as prophetically powerful as you are, you will sometimes be rejected by those you have served the most. What's incredible about this is that God announces to Samuel something that we all must know. He tells Samuel that their desire for a king was not that they were rejecting him personally. They were leaving the God that was leading him.

Often, when we are rejected by those we lead, we can internalize that rejection and provide the negativity of that emotion to find a permanent residence in our hearts. Now, we don't lead with as much enthusiasm as we did before. It's more of a burden now than a genuine pleasure. If the truth is told, we do want everyone to see our purpose in their lives. However, we must accept that there will always be people who won't see us as valuable or purposeful. Samuel would continue to have a purpose, just not in the life of the one he had anointed.

How many times as a leader have you been rejected by those you have anointed and laid your hands on? You can most likely recall the many that have come through the doors of your ministry or life and then compare them with the numbers that are with you today. Many of them have gone on to do great things for God, and I know you are glad about that. But that doesn't erase the feeling of their rejection of you when honor should have been their only response. Rejection is painful. There's no easy way for me to say that. It sucks.

When Jesus sends out His disciples, one of the things that He teaches them is about rejection. He says to them in Matthew 10:14, *"And whosoever shall not receive you, nor hear your words, when ye depart out of that house or city, shake off the dust of your feet."* Jesus knew that if we allow rejection to linger, it will hinder our ability to continue the assignment. He tells them to shake the dust off of their feet. What does that mean? Don't let the rejection of others stick to you. If you know anything about dirt, if you stand it in long enough, it will stick to the soles of your shoes. If this happens, the soil from one place will transfer to another. That's what's happened for many of us. We experienced great rejection but forgot to shake it off. So, when God brings new people for us to lead, we are still plagued with the dirt of that rejection. The people we are leading can feel it even if we never say it. How are you continuing your assignment after rejection?

Continuing your assignment being whole from rejection looks a certain way. It's not feeding people with a 30-foot spoon. Yes, I know that's what feels and sounds good, but that's not really the Word. Even as He teaches them what to do when they are rejected, He also teaches them what they should do when they are accepted. He says in Matthew 10:13, *"And if the house is worthy, let your peace come upon it: but if it be not worthy, let your peace return to you."* Look at that. There will always be people who reject you, but there will be many more who receive you in the power of the assignment you carry. Here's the blessing. The people that do receive you will develop into some of God's greatest servants, but you have to deal with the way you handle rejection first. I want to show you how Jesus handled it.

"In the beginning was the Word, and the Word was with God, and the Word was God. The same was in the beginning with God. All things were made by him; and without him was not anything made that was made. In him was life; and the life was the light of men. And the light shineth in darkness; and the darkness comprehended it not........He was in the world, and the world was made by him, and the world knew him not. He came unto his own, and his own received him not. But as many as received him, to them gave he power to become the sons of God, even to them that believe on his name: Which were born, not of blood, nor of the will of the flesh, nor of the will of man, but of God." **John 1:1-5, 9-13 KJV**

The above scriptures detail the foundational authority of

Jesus Christ and the mission He came to the earth to accomplish. In exquisite detail, we see His transference from divinity into a natural existence among those who would later discount Him as an earthly man without much significance or power. The Bible says that He was in the world, and the world knew Him not. Many of the people that He was sent to heal would reject Him. But the powerful thing about it was that at the end of the day, God would give Him those that would. Those individuals would receive the power to become everything their lives were created to be.

If you continue looking at the masses of people that reject you, you'll miss out on the opportunity to see those that are still in the dugouts of your life. You just don't need people in the stands. The audience in the stands leave. Sometimes, when they do, the applause they brought often goes with them. Now, you're standing on the field playing a game without the encouragement you thought you needed. However, we sometimes miss something crucial. Even when the game is over, and the audience has left to go back home, we are not left alone. God will always have people that are still in the dugout. Those are the people who got dirty with you when your challengers were playing hardball. They got down with you as your knees almost buckled under the pressure of the challenge and fight. They are like the Aaron's and Hur's that held up the hands of Moses when the battle was long and tiresome.

I want you to take a moment and possibly repent for discounting your dugout crew because of your disappointment of the audience that left you on the field. For most of us, we were never left alone. We just might not have as many with us now than we did before. However, that is about to change.

Even after raising disciples and garnering much support, Jesus again demonstrates to us, what we should do after being rejected. In John 6, the level of Jesus' teaching was about to take another turn. They had walked with him for some time, and God would need to shift the ranks to determine who would go along with him for the rest of the journey. Friends, before this next shift, there must be a sift. Often, when God is sifting our ranks, we feel as though we are not doing something right, being the best leader we can, or because of something that we have done.

But what God is doing is lightening our weight so that we can ascend higher.

As Jesus elevates His level of teaching, the Bible says that many begin to murmur and talk against what was being taught. Jesus knew within himself that they were offended and began questioning them. For most of them, they weren't interested in understanding. Their offense was already too strong. Those individuals decide not to walk with him anymore. Sometimes, even your most faithful aren't ready to take the next leg of the journey with you.

Jesus turns to the twelve that were remaining. His ranks had been cut, and now He looked at those left behind. If we were in His position, I could just imagine what would've been going on in our hearts. Wait! Some of us have experienced that, and some of us are right there now. Seeing what we used to have and the support that once surrounded us. Now, we are down to a little here or there. Also, sometimes the numbers aren't cut down, but the passionate support from those numbers isn't felt anymore. It's like individuals are coming to watch a movie but refuse to be participants or actors in our mission anymore.

He looks to the remnant and asks them a question that you have probably preached a few times, "Will you also go away?" In our hearts, we are always wondering whether we will be rejected or whether individuals still see us as a viable option. Some of you have asked yourself whether you should just send the people away? I want you to pause your decision and take this walk with me first.

Without hesitation, Peter declares, "Where shall we go? For you have the words of eternal life." God had left Jesus with a remnant that would do more than what the masses could've ever accomplished. Sometimes, when we are rejected, our immediate thought is to stop and turn back. Rarely do we ever pay attention to those who are left behind. Often, those who remain might have been those who weren't as boisterous as those who left or as polished, but I want to show you something.

Whenever there is space given for growth, the fruit will show up. Sometimes the remnant couldn't grow because the space in your life wouldn't allow it. You were cramped and without the time needed to cultivate your real army. So, without our permission, God makes the space we need to develop the leaders necessary for the next half of the assignment.

To provide a complete picture, let's pick back up on Samuel's journey as He moves beyond rejection and ministers to someone right in the middle of it. After King Saul displeased the Lord, God sent Samuel to the house of Jesse. God asks Samuel a pivotal question that I would like for us to unpack for a moment. He asks Samuel, *"How long will you mourn for Saul, seeing I have rejected him from reigning over Israel?"* What's important to note here is that this was the same Saul that God had once told Samuel to anoint, but now he is rejected and disqualified from leading God's people. God tells him to go to Jesse the Bethlehemite because He had provided himself a king among his sons.

God always has options. I know that we are the friends of God. Sometimes, we even feel as though we have God in our back pockets. However, we should all know that God can replace any one of us at a moment's notice. The truth is, right now, someone is being prepared to replace you. I know that doesn't make you feel good, but the mission of Christ won't be hindered because you choose not to obey Him. God always has someone that will. So, when God puts down one, He is always prepared to put up another. We see that very clear here in this passage. While Saul was being dethroned, God was anointing his replacement. But, guess what? Saul didn't know it. God was behind the scenes setting the stage for a new king while Saul was still on the throne.

Often, we look at the Body of Christ's landscape and envy those seated in authority. Many times, we have no clue who God intends to occupy those seats in the future. So, it's usually a good idea to honor, but never to idolize. God is the one that prepares kings, and He will use individuals like you to anoint and prepare them for service.

As we continue, one of the prevailing questions that I want to reverberate in your mind is, "Who am I choosing to develop?" Are you just choosing seemingly seated people, or are you looking beyond the seat and seeing something greater? If Samuel didn't know God, he would have continued to mourn the seat of Saul while disregarding the heart of God. Seeing the heart of God often will cause you to bypass those who are all together. You'll have to appreciate what they have to offer and choose to lay your hands on individuals whose treasures aren't seen yet. Can you do this? How well do you see treasures in dirty places?

Samuel arrives. Because of the role of the prophet, it wasn't very hard to tell that his arrival was an important visit. The Bible says that when Samuel arrives in the town, the elders wanted to make sure that he was coming in peace. They were trembling at the possibility that he was being sent to them with a word or assignment that would have done them harm, but this was not the case. Samuel informs them that he had come to sacrifice to the Lord. He then calls Jesse and his sons to the sacrifice.

I want to pause here and make a symbolism that I feel is vital to restoration and healing. For you to be the conduit of restoration in the life of anyone, you will have to make some sort of sacrifice. That sacrifice might be your reputation. It might be the way that others view you in light of who you have chosen to anoint, prepare or develop. It might even be the sacrificing of the fear you may have about the repercussions of doing so. Samuel had spoken to the Lord about that type of thing as well. He told the Lord that if Saul hears about what I am doing, he will kill me.

Too often, we refuse to heal and restore broken individuals because of fear. We'll even be talked out of doing what we know God has called us to do because of what our friends and colleagues will say. We have often been convinced out of embracing and developing some of the greatest gifts that will hit the earth. But I want you to watch out for individuals who talk you out of restoring others. Sometimes, your rejection will become their next appreciation. Yes! People will discourage you from healing others and will make them their new assignment in the next season. There are a few reasons for that. One of those reasons is because they see who you are. The other reason is that they know what the potential of the other individual is. If they can get them away from you, they can use the potential of the other individual for their benefit. That's how jealousy works.

I know you may not see yourself as anything super great, but others do, whether they tell you or not. They see who God has made you and the ability that He has given you. They know that you have the power to make others great, and in doing so, God will make your name just as great. So, the objective is to remove any viable students from your classroom. Who is a teacher without students? I think you see where I'm going with this. From this day forward, I want you to trust what you see in an individual, no matter how broken they may be today. They just might be another David that will usher in the kingdom of God.

As we look back at the story, Samuel has all of Jesse's sons to pass before him. The Bible doesn't say that Jesse knew what God had planned, yet he didn't invite David along when he was called to the sacrifice. The question is then posed, why not? Most likely, in Jesse's opinion, David might've not had much to offer to the occasion. It was more important for him to stay in the fields and tend to the sheep than to come to such an important event. See, Jesse's qualifications were probably based on what he could see and what he thought Samuel wanted to see. This was not how the Lord saw things at all.

God had already planned to use the least among them to become the greatest. I want you to begin evaluating how you see those around you. How are you distinguishing who God can use and, most of all, your role in developing them for the role God has designed.

Just think about it. His father was rejecting him. According to some Jewish thought, one of the reasons this may have been is that David was thought of as another man's child. If this is so, then, of course, Jesse would not have invited him. If we look into this, it might be why David wrote in Psalms 51:5, *"Behold, I was brought forth in iniquity and in sin did my mother conceive me."* In Psalms 69:8, he also says something interesting. He says, *"I have become a stranger unto my brethren and an alien unto my mother's children."*

Whether you choose to believe any of those connections or not, what's evident is that he was left behind. He was rejected. That sound's familiar as well, seeing our Lord was rejected and despised. So, it is no question that one of the major assignments of Christ through us is to find those who are rejected and broken and restore them to health. Remember, David was rejected, but he was a man after God's own heart.

Friends, it's effortless to anoint and develop those that are publicly acceptable. There's no hesitation in presenting those who have the look or the sound. However, God wants to raise individuals just like you to see deeper than that. Seeing deeper means that if I am to be used to heal and restore, I must see through the lens of Christ. How does God see them? And to take that a step further, how does God see you?

Restoration is a method that brings a person back to a particular state. So, in the context of this discussion, restoration isn't a place found in the natural. Restoration is a place that possibly the individual never understood they held spiritually.

There are millions of people walking around daily who have no clue of their eternal definition. When I speak of eternal definitions, I am talking about who they were before they were ever formed in the womb of their mother. The only thing they know is who they are and what they have become according to the world's standards.

As believers, this is a dangerous example to follow when choosing who to restore. God has not called us to heal individuals based on what the world says is acceptable. Before I move on, I want to make something clear. The church has a world too, and often that world doesn't follow the patterns of Christ either. We have, in many areas, adopted the way the world chooses instead of seeing the picture that God can only paint.

Just think about it. All of these sons are standing before the prophet Samuel parading their muscularity, stature, and honor. For a brief moment, even Samuel assumed that God's anointed was standing before him. See, even the most mature among us can be fooled to pick and choose based on outward appearance. Suddenly, God speaks to Samuel and rebukes him concerning how he was about to anoint a king. God reminds him that the way He saw individuals was not based on the outward appearance but the heart. It takes another level of discernment to know the heart because sometimes the external can be very loud. If you aren't careful, you'll disregard some individuals as noise when God has anointed them to be a sound that would carry His mission all over the earth.

After displaying his chosen sons, Samuel inquires if there was another son that he had not seen. Reluctantly, Jesse points out one son that was out in the fields. Samuel instructs him to bring the boy to him. That boy was David. When David comes before Samuel, he wasn't what he had expected. Immediately, the Lord speaks to him and tells him to arise and anoint him, for he is the one. I want to say this to you prophetically. God is about to anoint the least expected. Yes! There are individuals that we can't imagine will be used by God that will. Possibly, some people are watching you right now. They might assume that you will never get back up, be restored, healed, and elevated. They are liars. You, too, will become exactly who God has intended and will arise to levels that you can't even see for yourself.

The purpose of my taking a moment to share this illustration is to show you the power of hearing the voice of God in choosing to restore those who are rejected. The mere anointing of David did more for him than we could realize. After being sent to the fields and rejected by his family, God still saw him as someone great.

Sometimes, you can know you're great but still need the affirmation of someone else. This is what happened to David, and prayerfully this is what will happen for you. It is my prayer that God will appoint someone to come and anoint you. I know that our anointing comes from God and that this should be enough. It is. However, a validation comes as God dispatches his servants to go to others in a public display and announce their connection to Him and His will. In addition, there's a healing that occurs when we know that God has seen us, especially after man has hidden us.

Lastly, I want to share how God sends Ananias to us and sends us as Ananias to others. Later, as Saul's kingdom is being destroyed, God uses David to restore someone who was rejected and forgotten. This person's name was Mephibosheth.

Mephibosheth was the son of David's friend Jonathan and the grandson of King Saul. In 2 Samuel 4:4, the Bible shares that Mephibosheth becomes lame as his nurse drops him fleeing danger at five years old. His name consequently means "from the mouth of shame." This nurse was supposed to protect him, and because of fear, she injures him instead. Well, we could probably write one thousand sermons from that one thought, but we don't have time to stop there.

For years, Mephibosheth is rejected from anything pertaining to the kingdom and is forgotten in a place called Lo-debar. Lo-debar wasn't the town where the upper echelon of society dwelt. It would, in our times, be considered the ghetto. How could seed with a royal heritage be found in a place like this? Well, there are so many examples of this in our day and time. These individuals have the treasure of the kingdom within but feel left by the wayside and without anyone to restore them. But little do they know; God is about to send you.

As the story unfolds, David is now in power, and his kingdom is united. He remembers the promise he made to Mephibosheth's father, Jonathan, and begins to inquire of any people who are left from that lineage. To his surprise, he discovers that there was someone still alive from the house of Saul.

In haste, David makes his way to where Mephibosheth was. In great shame, Mephibosheth humbly lowers his head at the majesty he saw when he looked at King David. He calls himself a dead dog. He had long lost the hope of being at the king's table and had accepted his fate. However, God had sent someone for him.

"Don't be afraid," David said to him, "for I will surely show you kindness for the sake of your father, Jonathan. I will restore to you all the land that belonged to your grandfather Saul, and you will always eat at my table." **2 Samuel 9:7**

In one day, Mephibosheth had gone from being rejected and forgotten to being restored, sitting at the king's table with inheritance and power. The powerful lesson in this is that God used someone who had once been rejected to restore him. Many of you reading this are leaders who have experienced the pain of rejection. Many of you have risen through the ranks and are now feasting at tables of abundance and health.

I want you to remember something. One day, God sent you an Ananias that anointed your head with oil giving you the confidence to journey ahead. Now, God depends on you to do that for someone else. Find God's lost treasures. They might be lame, wounded, and discouraged, but you have exactly what they need to arrive at restoration and be the kings and priests that God has purposed them to be. You are Ananias!

4

"I CAN'T SEE"

NAVIGATING BLIDING SITUATIONS

The extraordinary thing about God is that He has an incredible way of bringing together people that would've otherwise stayed apart. He knows exactly how to orchestrate events to bring connections and also lessons. Yes! When God connects the opposites of anything, He intends on teaching both sides something powerful. Have you ever heard of someone long before you met them? And, based on what you heard, you had no desire of ever being their friend? Well, this is how this story begins.

Saul was nothing but a terror in the eyes of all that had believed in Jesus Christ. He wasn't someone that they looked to invite to their next gathering or meal. They had no intention of ever crossing paths with him, but God had a plan that would outwit them and also show them that the way He chooses is not like man. What a joy that should be to your ears? Sometimes, when we look at specific individuals, we can't fathom them ever being used by God or ever touching our lives in a significant way. Most likely, that is what someone was thinking about you once. And just look at you now!

As this extraordinary story begins, we see the powerful display of Saul's authority as he is sanctioned by the high priest, giving him letters with authorization to take prisoner any individual found believing in Jesus Christ. For you to understand the zeal of Saul of Tarsus, you would have to understand his background. Saul was a learned man in the Hebrew scriptures and had sat at the feet of the rabbi Gamaliel to begin an extensive study into the law. He was not a novice by any means and was zealous in executing its punishments in every way possible. However, he would soon learn that the Jesus he intended to persecute was not an ordinary man. He was Christ, full of power and authority in heaven, earth, and hell.

Saul, being full of rage against the Lord's disciples, comes close to Damascus when suddenly a brilliant light pauses his pursuit. Isn't this something? Often, we are so full of zeal that we miss the target of who we are called to be. In Saul's efforts to stop the Lord's disciples, he had no clue that he would become one of them. The call of God on his life wasn't something new to God. It was who he was born to be. He just didn't know it.

At some point, you were just like Saul. You were zealous in what you thought was right and would soon find out that you weren't. Sometimes, even as leaders, we can do something for so long we convince ourselves that it is the right path. It might be in the way we have done ministry or how we have handled the people we were called to lead. Unfortunately, often, it takes something drastic for us ever to acknowledge our wrongdoing. I'll be the first to tell you that you don't have to continue on any path that doesn't lead you directly to Christ.

One of the greatest enemies against any leader is pride, and as the Word of God tells us, in Proverbs 16:18, *"Pride goes before destruction and a haughty spirit before a fall."* See, pride blinds us from ever believing that it can happen to us. We are convinced that if we are smart enough, careful enough, and cunning enough, we can continue doing what we are doing even when it goes against God's ultimate plan for our lives. Friends, this cannot be further from the truth.

Whenever pride is in operation in your leadership, it has the potential of killing all of your efforts and pushing out the valuable help that God has sent to advance your assignment. When is the last time that you have evaluated your level of pride? I know that we want to think we are as humble as they come, but those around us might not believe the same. We are often blinded by our ambition in ministry that we forget that *God resists the proud and gives grace to the humble* (1 Peter 5:5). What we must recognize is that our exaltation must come from God. If it comes any other way, it will be soon cut down by the Christ we so vehemently say we serve. If anything is to be exalted in your ministry, let that be Him.

One of the things I have learned from platform ministry is that it makes us feel like celebrities. We have people who wait for us at the doors of our sanctuaries, audiences who can't wait to hear us speak, individuals who are faithful sowers, and those who would do anything they can to support us. However, sometimes, all of those things have a way of building up to something that God hates, pride. Your platform doesn't matter if your character is jacked up.

It's dangerous to be a prideful leader. The importance of my time sharing this with you is to show you a striking connection between brokenness and the results of pride. Yes! There are some instances where we have been hurt, not because of the efforts of another individual, though. We are damaged sometimes because of traps we willingly walked into because we were prideful.

Let's begin by talking about how sinful pride is and how it creates unhealthy growth in your leadership ability. Pride is an attitude of the heart and is expressed through an exaggerated need for attention to oneself, abilities, accomplishments, achievements, status, or possessions. It is likened to the soul's disease and is most certainly the beginning stages of a myriad of sin and dysfunction. If you take a moment to think about it, pride is the beginning and the final form of all sinful acts. Pride is also the direct opposite of humility. Remember, humility is what God desires from all that believe in him, and most certainly, the desired characteristic in those called to lead His people.

Pride is a crucial topic in this chapter because when you are filled with it as a leader, failures in your leadership are always someone else's fault but your own. You cannot ever fully acknowledge its results, and those you lead are constantly responsible for what you have done.

One of the things that must happen if you are ever to be fully healed and restored is a renewed responsibility for what might've gone wrong at your hands. We know that the enemy inspires all evil, but sometimes, we are not good soldiers at stopping what he introduces. Most of the time, we are entirely unaware that we are prideful. This lack of awareness is the breeding ground for future failure and destruction.

"See, I will make you small among the nations; you will be utterly despised. The pride of your heart has deceived you, you who live in the clefts of the rocks and make your home on the heights, you who say to yourself, "Who can bring me down to the ground?"

Obadiah 1:2-3

Deception arrives in the heart because of pride. It will mask itself in some of our most published achievements with an effort to cement its path in our life. Unfortunately, many of us don't realize we are full of it until we have fallen and failed. According to Proverbs 11:2, Pride will always lead to disgrace. Why? Because it teaches us to always keep our eyes on ourselves rather than on God. So, ultimately, pride causes spiritual blindness and inevitable destruction.

Another thing about pride is that pride can be long-lasting. It can form a sense of invincibility around you, and because nothing harmful has occurred yet, it can make you think that it will never happen. This cannot be more wrong, as we know.

When we think about King David, the man the Bible says was after God's own heart. We can see clearly that he was a leader that dealt with the sin of Pride. Even after God snatched him from obscurity and made him be noted among the greatest, he too was overtaken by pride which caused him to lose what he greatly desired.

There was a notable event that we can look at concerning the pride that caused David to fail in his rule. This event is his dealings with Bathsheba. It takes tons of pride to look upon another man's wife, order her husband on the front line, take her as yours, and then to assume there would be no consequence. As the story goes, God sends Nathan the Prophet to David in 2 Samuel 12. Nathan begins to tell David a report of a rich and poor man. Of course, the rich man had many possessions and goods, but the poor man had only one lamb. As the rich man is entertaining a traveler who had come to visit, he prepares a meal. In the act of dominance, he doesn't take a lamb from the many in his flock. Instead, he takes the only lamb that the poor man had in his possession.

As David hears about these events, he is full of anger and rage. Who would do such a thing? I'm sure this is what David thought. Being full of retribution, he commands that the man that had done this egregious act die and that the lamb is restored four times over to the poor man. Immediately, the Prophet Nathan declares this in 2 Samuel 12:7-14: "Then Nathan said to David, "You are the man! This is what the Lord, the God of Israel, says: 'I anointed you king over Israel, and I delivered you from the hand of Saul. I gave your master's house to you and your master's wives into your arms. I gave you all Israel and Judah. And if all this had been too little, I would have given you even more. Why did you despise the word of the Lord by doing what is evil in his eyes? You struck down Uriah the Hittite with the sword and took his wife to be your own. You killed him with the sword of the Ammonites. Now, therefore, the sword will never depart from your house, because you despised me and took the wife of Uriah the Hittite to be your own.

"This is what the Lord says: "Out of your own household, I am going to bring calamity on you. Before your very eyes, I will take your wives and give them to one who is close to you, and he will sleep with your wives in broad daylight. You did it in secret, but I will do this thing in broad daylight before all Israel.'" Then David said to Nathan, "I have sinned against the Lord."

Nathan replied, "The Lord has taken away your sin. You are not going to die. But because by doing this you have shown utter contempt for the Lord, the son born to you will die."

Wow! What a complete turn of events. Pride will lead you directly into a trap. David, in all of his splendor and majesty, felt untouchable. He had the woman that he wanted and now was expecting a son. However, the penalty of pride would cost him severely.

Another thing that I want you to notice about pride in leadership is that we can often see no wrong in what we do but can clearly identify it in others. Even in listening to the detailed story by the Prophet Nathan, David still didn't see himself as the character. How many times have you heard a situation dealing with someone else and become enraged? But soon understood that you had done and participated in the same act at one time or another? Did you remain angry and offer the same punishment for yourself? Or, did you go your way and forget what you saw in yourself?

What I am hoping that you see in this story is that pride is dangerous. David did not acknowledge his sin until pride had done its best work with him. He never thought that there would be a consequence for it until it was too late.

Leaders, when is the last time you prayed about the possible pride in your heart? David is now a broken leader, not because of the fault of anyone. He was broken because of the penalty of his own pride. If you don't deal with it, you will find yourself losing the very thing that was supposed to be your gain and for God's glory.

As we continue our discussion from Acts 9, Saul is now blinded by the brilliant light of Christ. Doesn't God have a way of stopping us when we're on the wrong path? Often, it will look like a slowing down of funds, dwindling of our congregations, lowered engagement invitations, or just the fading away of popularity. Now, some of those events are because of the enemy's assignment against our progress, but often they can be the consequences of going on the wrong path.

Saul wasn't the only character in the Bible who was paused in his pursuit. Do you remember Balaam and how God told him not to curse His people, but yet he overrode the word of the Lord and continued his way? The Bible details in Numbers 22:21-39 that God sent an angel to stand in the path with a sword drawn in his hands to stop Balaam from going any further. Unfortunately, just like some of us, he couldn't see it, but the donkey he was riding did. Every time the donkey attempted to go another way, Balaam would hit him and punish his disobedience. Having been beaten enough, God opened the donkey's mouth and explained to him why he was being rerouted and what would happen if he continued his way.

Friends, there have been so many incidents that we could recall in our own lives and leadership, where God has allowed certain events to happen to reroute us. Often, we never thought that God caused the events and that He allowed them to happen to get our attention and direct us on a more straightforward path. This is what was happening to Saul in Acts 9. It was time for Saul to acknowledge his ordained calling and to begin using his knowledge and gifts for the glory of God.

Aren't you ready to do more for God? For many of us, we have only scratched the surface of our calling. We are just like Saul. We have been zealous in doing what we have known, but God now requires us to do more. In God directing us to do more and to see things differently, he sometimes blinds the former way we have seen something.

Have you ever discovered that you suddenly don't think of things the same way you did before? Or, you can't process mentally as sharp as you have before in a particular area? Sometimes, the best way God can get us to think differently is to block the way we see things. Saul has been blinded.

I CAN'T SEE!

If you are reading this book, there is something that I fully believe. Firstly, I believe that you are a leader in motion. Now, some of you are saying, "No, I'm not. I'm broken." While that might be true and your current reality, there is something more significant going on in you. There is upward mobility occurring in your life that you may not be aware of. Just as God dealt with Saul, God is most likely dealing with you. I'm not saying that you are full of pride or are doing anything that is going against the cause of Christ. What I am saying is that God is redirecting you on a clearer path. The truth is, our current approaches in many areas haven't brought us the level of fruitfulness and fulfillment as we have desired. The lack of satisfaction is what causes regret, resentment, and many times rage.

Can you imagine the anger that filled the heart of Saul as he thought about the multitudes of people that had so much joy because of this man named Jesus Christ? In his own heart, the law had never given him that much hope. Often, when we are leading and not experiencing what others are, it can form a subtle layer of rage within us. This rage is demonstrated sometimes in manipulation, the demand for honor, control, etc. If you are angry as a leader today, it might be because you have not fully embraced the light that is causing you now to become blind.

Guess what? God never intended for Saul to be permanently blind. He wanted to expose him to a greater way of seeing things, and He understood that Saul had to become humble first. Listen, friends, the best way to become humble is to do it yourself. When God humbles us, His methods are most inconvenient and come at the worst times. God will allow your star to rise and your platforms to increase, and right when you think you are at the pinnacle of power, here comes the light. One way or another, God is going to be glorified.

Saul was in motion but now can't see. What happens when you are a leader in momentum and are blindsided by an issue that you had no idea would occur? While Saul was a leader full of pride and the wrong zeal, some of you are God's most treasured servants who are doing the best that you can. Suddenly, you discover that while you are pleasing God, an issue arises that totally blindsides you and takes away your focus.

One of the most desperate and humiliating cries of a leader is when you have to admit to yourself and others, "I CAN'T SEE!" If this has ever occurred in your life, you know exactly what I mean. At this point, you have options. You can continue acting like you can see the path forward, or you can humble yourself and admit that you have lost your sight.

Friends, there is a myriad of circumstances that arise in

the life of a leader that takes away our sight. Sometimes, it's simply unfortunate circumstances. Often, it's losing the support we thought we had. Or, it might be personal issues that prick the very heart of who we think we are in God. All of those instances can blind us.

In addition to accepting your blindness in certain events, you are now having to face announcing to those around you that you can't see as well. Do you now know the importance of humility and the increasing opportunity of pride here? As leaders, we are taught to see afar off and lead no matter what, but one of your greatest opportunities to display your leadership is showing the people what humility looks like.

Saul was blinded while traveling with others. The individuals that he was traveling with were probably under his command. They were looking to him for direction because he was the one with authority. What do you do when you can't see, but people depend on you to lead? You humble yourself, trust that those you lead will see the power in your humility and see in the areas you currently can't. Do you see how that cuts away at the enemy's plan for you to remain prideful? Saul had to now depend on the men following him to take the lead until he could see for himself.

As a leader, you can mend your brokenness by trusting in those placed around you. Now, I'm not telling you to trust everyone. We all know this is not the right thing to do. However, I am saying that you must trust those that are divinely placed around you for support. What's the use in having God sent people if you will not use them to see in the areas that you can't? Leaders, we don't catch everything.

Throughout scripture, we see how God used the prophetic to steer not only the heart of King's but the sight of King's. Remember, you are a leader in motion, and every time you don't use the sight of those around you, there's a possibility that you'll be slowed down or even stopped when your issues blind you. Yes! We all have personal problems, and when those personal issues become too weighty, if we don't have the right people around us to guide us, the ministry will lose its ground and speed.

As Jesus presents himself to Saul, He says something

compelling. He asks him the question, "Saul, Saul, why do you persecute me?" In all of the great things that we do, we must consistently search for areas within our soul that are persecuting the cause of Christ. Often, we are so broken at life or the events in ministry that our attitudes and hearts become hardened. If you didn't realize it, a hardened heart is a persecution of the Christ that comes to change hearts. Stop! Take a moment to repent for any area of your heart that has become hard to His direction in your life and the way He would have you to lead His people.

After Jesus' introduction, Jesus informs Saul that it is dangerous to kick against the prick. He tells him that even though his efforts were bold that they would never win against him. Saul is now blind and humbled. There's only one option from here. That one option is to submit.

As you read this, prayerfully, you are deciding to submit even more than you have. We must acknowledge that some of the pains we have experienced haven't been because of the devil. They have been a result of us not being fully submissive to the assignment of Christ in our lives and the purpose that He has called us to fulfill. Jesus still wants a yes out of you.

Another interesting facet of this story is that the men that followed Saul didn't hear the voice of Jesus speaking to him. They couldn't interpret the sounds they heard to affirm Saul's new direction or understand why he could no longer see.

There will be times in your leadership that you will have to take directives alone and trust that those you lead will know your track record in making necessary transitions. Now, Saul was about to take a drastic turn from what they had known. When you are leading after the heart of Christ, it's always a good idea to update your flock on your willingness to do whatever Christ demands. Sometimes, it will be a smooth turn to the left, while other times, it will be a hard turn to the right. But, whatever you do, follow Christ.

5

CHOOSING THE RIGHT ANANIAS

A s this powerful story continues in Acts 9, Jesus tells Saul to go into the city and that he would receive further instructions. The men who were traveling with him are speechless and amazed. Oh, how the mighty are fallen. Throughout history, we have seen the elevation of extraordinary gifts to the Body of Christ, and unfortunately, we have also seen many of their falls and failures. This view is not to bring any level of condemnation but to show all of us the constant need for Christ's direction and guidance in our life. In this chapter in the life of Saul, he needed Jesus now more than ever before. Don't we all?

One of the things about brokenness is that it gets us back to the heart of Christ and our constant need for him. See, true restoration feels like you're being stripped. The fading away of reputation and applause can make you seem like you've lost something when you've really won someone greater. You're now nothing to those who once knew you but are now everything to people who don't even know your name. Sometimes, you can be stripped but helped in a more remarkable way at the same time.

One of the sobering realities of true restoration is that it will require you to zero out your ego. Often, it is not that we don't want to become whole. We just don't want to let go of what others think our strength and wholeness come from. You are more than the coat you wear. Be willing to let it go, so you can become more than what others ever expect.

Do you remember Joseph? He was the son of his father's

old age. To display great love, his father made him a coat of many colors. His father loved him, but his brothers despised him. If things couldn't have gotten worse, or better depending on how you see it, they hated him more because of his dreams. What's so interesting about this was that the plan of God for his life was far more significant than a coat. However, it symbolized the father's love for him in a way that could be seen. To kill the dream of Joseph, his jealous brothers throw him in a pit, but before they do this, they take away the thing that made him most proud. They stripped him of his coat and dipped it in blood. The life source of anything is in the blood. Now, this bloody coat represented two things to all that saw it. It represented Joseph's dreams of the future, as well as the end of the hope that it would come to pass. At least that's what they thought.

There will be moments in your restoration process that will look just like that. Sometimes, you will lose a lot during the process but seem as though God will require more. The audience of spectators will grow, and now everyone has a front-row seat of what they think is your demise. You're stripped and apparently in a place that very few think you're going to come out of. Fortunately, this was not the plan of God for Joseph, and it certainly isn't the plan of God for you. I want you to allow God to remove any external symbolism that might hinder the process from continuing the way He has designed. There will be some that won't understand. They'll think that God has left you or that you have missed the mark. The truth is that some of us have, some of us will, and some of us are simply experiencing the healing process after disappointments that were beyond our control.

I want you for a moment to think about the process that EMTs take when they are evaluating anyone who has experienced great trauma. I'm sure that you have watched this scenario on a television show, or you may have even experienced it first-hand. Just picture it. They are wheeling that person into the emergency room. They see blood but sometimes don't know where it's coming from. What's the first thing they do? They cut off the person's clothing to better look or expose the body's area that needs the most help. Under normal circumstances, this would be humiliating. But, when you are fighting for your life and wanting help, clothes is the least of your concern.

What's my point in sharing that with you? It's to show you that when restoration and healing are your ultimate goal, you are okay with temporary bouts of humiliation as long as you come out of it better and with the help you need. Joseph would come out of his process not only with the help he needed but in a better position to help those who needed it the most.

I don't for one moment believe that all of the men who were following Saul trusted his new direction. That could not have been the best feeling, but his loss of reputation in one area was the building of Christ's name in another. What is more important to you? Is it more important for you to prove to people how strong you are or how healed you are? Or are you more concerned now with displaying what a grace-filled leader looks like?

Later in Paul's (Saul's) ministry, he would teach us the power of walking in the grace of God through our weaknesses and broken places. These areas are sometimes intimate places that go well beyond the knowledge of anyone, but they are targets of the grace of

God that strengthens us through them. So, what's more valuable in this season? Your reputation or God's grace?

Some of you thought this book would be a diary of a mad leader or the journal of what people do to hurt us. As you have read, this is so much more than that. When our hearts have become disjointed, our passions lead us away from the light of Christ. It is then that the door is opened to make the wrong decisions, be unwise in who and what we connect with or to become blinded by pride and not see destruction as it approaches. The heart is most deceitful and is not to be trusted unless it is centered in Christ Jesus.

The Bible makes a special note to share with us in Acts 9:9 that Saul is blind and doesn't eat for three days. It was possibly his shock in being placed in such a situation that took away his appetite. I'm sure he never considered that the power he had heard about was real, and even if he did, he might've not ever thought that it could affect him. All of us have experienced the sharp edges of the sword of the Word. Its razor-sharp ability cuts into the most hidden place within our hearts, exposing every area that we refuse to submit to Him.

It will amaze you the number of leaders guiding congregations who are not submitted fully to the Word of God. We study messages that don't personally convict us of hiding that place from God. You can never hide from God. It doesn't matter how famous you have become or how wise you are in your own eyes. When it's time for God to stop you, He will.

Jesus instructs Saul to go into town and to wait for further instructions. At the very same time, God is now beginning to introduce the focal character (other than Jesus) in this book. His name is Ananias.

"In Damascus, there was a disciple named Ananias. The Lord called to him in a vision, "Ananias!" "Yes, Lord," he answered. The Lord told him, "Go to the house of Judas on Straight Street and ask for a man from Tarsus named Saul, for he is praying. In a vision, he has seen a man named Ananias come and place his hands on him to restore his sight." **Acts 9:10-11**

Can you imagine the joy that arose in the heart of Ananias when the Lord began speaking to him? I'm sure that he had no clue about the awesome assignment given to him and the courage and boldness it would take for him to complete the task.

Leaders, many times, God will lead you just like He is about to lead Ananias. You'll have to choose to obey God in restoring an individual in light of who they are and what they have done. God has a great way of choosing who we despise and using them for His glory. Often, many leaders reject God's chosen not because the individual is unworthy but because of personal insecurities and the need to be accepted among our colleagues and friends.

Some of you are just now making a name for yourselves, but maybe that is the problem. In this culture-driven church, we have missed out on the principle that God introduced to Abraham in Genesis 12. He tells Abraham that if you obey me in the instructions I give you, I will make your name great. Abraham now has a choice to make. He can either stay among the people that made him feel comfortable or become inconvenienced by obeying God.

Can you fathom what was going on in the minds and mouths of the people around Abraham? He was in a town where his father had wealth, and he had the security of prominence. However, God wanted to do something more significant in his life and through his obedience. You must understand that every time God leads you to develop or restore anyone, He is doing something for that individual and you at the same time. You build up your credit with God as you walk by faith in restoring those that He loves. Friends, God wants to make your name great, but it will never happen if you don't begin to obey him by making His name great first.

One of the things that I love about Jesus and His assignment on earth is that He wasn't concerned with His earthly reputation. He knew who He was and was fully aware of what He was born to do. There were times when His father used Him to do miraculous things, and He would order them not to make mention of it, although many didn't listen.

When He was brought before those in power, and they attempted to bait Him by asking Him if He was what they had heard, He simply said, "You said that." See, He wasn't concerned about what others thought about him, as long as He fulfilled His assignment. No one around

Him was more important than His father, and according to scripture, He did all things to please Him (John 8:29).

Just think about it. Every time Jesus interacted with anyone, it went against what those who should've known God thought. Sometimes even the most mature miss God. When the woman who was caught in adultery was paraded by the men who she slept with, Jesus cared not what they thought. In John 8:7, He simply wrote on the ground and announces to them, *"He who is without sin cast the first stone."*

Another instance of Jesus restoring someone is the passage that we find in Mark 5. There we see how Jesus dealt with the woman with the issue of blood. According to the law, this woman should've been nowhere near the crowd. Instead of Jesus being concerned with what people thought about him, he still healed her and allowed the virtue that had the power to heal to do its job.

What am I saying to you? There is so much that God has invested in you as a leader. There's so much more that you can do to assist the cause of Christ, but sometimes we are swayed away from embracing individuals because of what others would think. Beloved friends, prayerfully, God is dealing with your heart right now concerning any individual that you have shunned based on the thoughts of individuals that should have known better.

Take a moment to consider Saul. As he was developed, he sat under the feet of one of the most knowledgeable priests. He was humble and submitted to his teaching and instructions. Be careful how you sandblast people, especially when they have been under the careful tutelage of leaders who should have advised them better. Every Saul isn't in the world. They're just in the wrong hands! What must be understood is that you can have a divine purpose but be in the WRONG HANDS! There could be so much more change in the world if we can just get people to the RIGHT PEOPLE.

Suppose you think about your journeys toward restoration. In that case, many of you can attest that there have been times when you might have joined a fellowship and organization with the desire to be healed and restored truly but quickly discovered that you were just used as a number for a Facebook post or ministry biography. It's not that your intention was off. It was just that you were in the wrong hands.

Sometimes, our efforts to touch the lives of everyone we come in contact with are pure. However, I want you to know that you don't have what it takes to heal everyone. Now, I know that statement flies in the face of every ounce of pride we have, but it's the truth. There will be instances where you will have to send individuals to another leader or another ministry. It doesn't mean that you aren't just as powerful, but not every leader carries the same skillset. Healing and restoration is a grace and before you further damage someone, be willing to send them to the right place for the healing they need. Be ready to drop them down at the feet of Jesus before you drop them, further damaging the area they need healing in the most. Often, when we don't humble ourselves in this area, we progress the hurt and pain the individual has already experienced. It's okay to say, "I can't help you, but I know someone who can." Everyone needs the right Ananias. You do as well!

CHOOSING THE RIGHT ANANIAS

When researching the Bible, you will see that there was

more than one Ananias. Before this book, some of you had never heard of this particular Ananias. You had only heard of the Ananias that lied and not the Ananias that restored. See, the Ananias that most of us are more familiar with was one who lied to the Holy Ghost as he was speaking to the Apostle Peter in Acts 5. The Apostle Peter asks him, *"Ananias, how is it that Satan has so filled your heart that you have lied to the Holy Spirit?"* This Ananias didn't realize that even though he was speaking to a man, he was lying to the Holy Spirit.

In every great house, there are vessels of all kinds. What must be understood and accepted is not all leaders have your best interest in heart. Some leaders will prey on your weaknesses, while others just want to use you for their gain. This Ananias was a leader who lied.

Let's pause here for a moment and talk about an example of this. In Acts 16-21, we find that Paul and Silas are going to the house of prayer when suddenly there appears this woman who was a slave. Now, this was no ordinary slave girl. The Bible says that she had a spirit of divination. She was able to tell the future, but she didn't do it for free. Her owners would use her to make money, bringing them great gain.

As we all know, all of us are born with gifts according to the need of God. I absolutely believe that there were gifts inside her that God wanted to use, but when a gift is placed in the wrong hands, it becomes perverted. This was the case here in scripture, according to my thoughts.

Because she was a slave, it's not like she could escape the control of her owners. She was in the wrong hands and used for the gain of those who controlled her. Countless gifted individuals in the Body of Christ are under the careful tutelage of the wrong Ananias. They are being used, but it's not for the glory of God. It is for the fame and benefit of those they are submitted to.

As the Bible continues sharing, this woman begins to follow Paul and his company. For many days she follows them declaring, *"These men are servants of the Most-High God, who are proclaiming to you the way of salvation!"*. Paul becomes aggravated. I want to point out that what she was saying was indeed true, but her delivery method was used to taunt them publicly. Paul has had enough and commands the spirit out of the girl, and immediately she was set free. She was now in the right hands.

Here's where things become interesting. The people who owned the girl became infuriated because they were now out of her money-making ability. They were perfectly okay with her being possessed with a demon, as long as they benefited from her efforts. See, when you are in the hands of the wrong Ananias, your freedom isn't their priority. They will lie and control you only to use your gifts, talents, and abilities for their gain. You must get free.

One notable characteristic that is particularly prone to leadership is dishonesty. Often, they are in a place of authority, and their lies become manageable because of the people who enable them. Unfortunately, once a leader has become successful in lying, it is hard to stop. One lie just piles onto another making it a slippery slope to overcome.

So, our first example of the wrong Ananias is a leader who lies. A leader who lies will ultimately hurt the individuals who come to them for healing and restoration, and they will become a stain on the mission of Christ on the earth. This type of leader doesn't lie alone. As we can see in the story of this Ananias, he is married to a woman named Saphira, who helps him lie. She knew that what he had planned to tell the Apostle Peter wasn't the truth. Pause! I wonder if their conversation was pre-planned or if they just simply behaved in a usual manner for them. See, when you choose this type of Ananias, it's hard to decipher between a slip-up and the actual character that they are made of.

In addition to their spouse, this type of Ananias must have a loyal group of followers. These followers are also fully aware of the lying capability of their leader and the harm and damage that they pose to hurting individuals. This crowd of followers is sometimes dismissive concerning the hurt details by others and will do everything in their power to hush any news of the damage the leader has caused. This silencing assists this type of leader continue growing their flock and gaining credibility from other leaders. I'm not saying the other leaders are complicit, but one of the things that makes other leaders stand in awe is a growing congregation because you have to be doing something right for your church to grow, right? And let's not talk about the signs and wonders. Often, we assume that because God heals someone in our churches or does something great through us, that He is personally endorsing us as a person. This cannot be further from the truth. God has a way of using an individual for His purpose just to get to another person's need. It has nothing to do with us. It has everything to do with Him. This is why we must all evaluate our hearts even though God is using us in any way.

Another characteristic of this type of leader is their ability to make individuals feel important or special. This tactic is beneficial when a leader is trying to attract an individual to their ministry or organization. They'll make you feel undervalued where you are with the hope of becoming recognized in the congregation they lead. Sadly, when this occurs, individuals discover that they have been used in a game they had no clue was already in progress.

This type of lying leader also uses their charm and charisma to attract the broken. They have the appropriate skills and personality that win their followers' love while lowering any guard the individual might have up. They'll use their charm to throw off a person's intuition concerning any behavior that might've been a red flag.

Another increasingly harmful characteristic of this type of Ananias is that they will use their force and the force of those around them to bully anyone who opposes or confronts their lies. Often, they'll use the dramatics of ministry, anointing, smoke, and mirrors to make others feel as though God is with them and that harm will come on a person if they are confronted. Friends, this is the WRONG ANANIAS!

Secondly, I want to talk to you about another Ananias that is found in Acts 23:1-2. This Ananias was a high priest in Jerusalem during Paul's early ministry. He was appointed by Herod Agrippa and was known for his cruelty and brutality. During Paul's trial in Jerusalem before the Sanhedrin council, he becomes enrages by Paul's words and orders him to be struck on the mouth. When this occurs, Paul says something that I want to use as the focal point of our discussion about this type of Ananias. Here's what Paul says, *"God will strike you, you whitewashed wall! You sit there to judge me according to the law, yet you violate the law by commanding that I be struck."* Acts 23:3

Once Paul realized that he was speaking to the high priest, he apologized. As Paul continued his defense, things became increasingly volatile, and Paul was escorted into protective custody. There was now a plot to murder him, and this Ananias was most likely involved. This type of Ananias isn't very spiritual at all. They are more Judgmental than they are Christlike.

Fortunately, you are reading this book and not a service where you have to testify. However, all of us can recall a time where we have been judged. Some of those instances were because of things that we knew we did incorrectly. Just like the woman who was caught in the act of adultery. The truth of the allegation wasn't the question—the authority of the men who brought her before Jesus was. See, sometimes, when dealing with this type of Ananias, they usurp the authority of Jesus Christ and execute their form of Jesus justice. This type of leader encourages a person to be ostracized, mocked, abused by fellow parishioners making them an outcast in a place they sought refuge and support.

In Galatians 6:1, the Bible teaches us this, *"Brothers, if anyone is caught in any transgression, you who are spiritual should restore him in a spirit of gentleness. Keep watch on yourself, lest you too be tempted."* With such a stern warning, you would think every leader would strive to obey its guidance, but that doesn't happen all of the time.

Often, when a leader loses sight of their frailty, they can become high-minded about the situations that they might one day find themselves in. In your past, have you ever boldly asserted that something would never happen to you? How you would never be caught in a particular situation? Or, how someone should have known better? And then, here comes life. This type of Ananias judges a person for something, sentencing them while doing the same thing they have just punished someone else about.

This Ananias also loves to do things publicly. They don't use confidentiality as a method of securing restoration. These are the types of leaders that always correct and rebuke in public. Their assertion of power publicly is often used to show force or violence in their congregations and organizations.

Whenever a person is seeking restoration, public humiliation is never God's way of building them back up.

God always encourages us to deal with individuals the same way Christ would have dealt with them in the Word. Public judgments concerning the failure of people were never a method that Jesus used to bring people back to God.

A judgmental leader will never see their faults, and because of this, you will find it very difficult to get them to understand and have compassion for yours. Let's look at what Jesus says about this.

"How can you say to your brother, Brother, let me take out the speck that is in your eye when you yourself do not see the log that is in your own eye? You hypocrite, first take the log out of your own eye, and then you will see clearly to take out the speck that is in your brother's eye." **Luke 6:42**

Listen, as a leader, I know the importance of sometimes having hard conversations with those you lead. However, those conversations must always be approached while being Christlike and, through the lens of considering oneself, lest you fall into the same situation because of your unrighteous judgment concerning someone else *(Luke 6:37).*

Lastly, we pick back up where we left off. The final Ananias is the Ananias, not that lied, not that judged, but that restored. In Acts 9:11, Jesus instructs Ananias where to go and that there would be a man named Saul of Tarsus. Immediately, he knew exactly who God was sending him to. He begins to tell the Lord all the things that he had heard about this man and how fearful he was concerning the cruelty that he displayed.

Can you imagine the position he was now in? Ananias had to overcome his fear while demonstrating the power of God to someone that made him afraid. Friends, there will be times when you will have to stand in the face of everyone that has made you fearful or frustrated. Your stand isn't about you preparing to fight but about you getting positioned to heal. It takes nothing to heal your friends, but what about your foes? Are you still as strong in the Lord as you thought?

Even when considering who you choose as your Ananias, I want you to realize that sometimes the Ananias you seek isn't the Ananias you should select. Selecting the most popular individual to walk you through your restorative process might not be the best fit. Think about this. The

Lord could've spoken to any of the other Apostles to find Saul. He didn't. He chooses someone the Bible says was full of integrity and had a good report among the people. Sometimes, when we seek to be restored, we must be honest in why we choose specific individuals.

Sometimes, it's not that we really want to be healed and restored. Sometimes, it's because we want to borrow someone's name until ours is cleaned up. This practice is manipulative and disgraceful to the purpose of God in our lives. God didn't send any of the celebrity Apostles to Saul. He sent someone who was a servant and had a good name among the people. A bad name can never restore a lousy name to health. Choose the right Ananias!

As the story continues, Ananias overcomes his fear and goes to Saul after the Lord tells him how chosen Saul is and what an instrument he would be to Him. God had a more excellent plan, and Ananias was a vital part of it coming to pass.

As a leader, you will have to take some bold steps in obeying God. Often, you will have to bypass the rumors and truths about individuals to do it. The obedience of this Ananias would be the catalyst in Saul becoming one of the scripture's most profound writers. Fear almost gripped him, but faith would give him the courage to lay hands on who would undoubtedly impact lives and generations to come. Your one act of faith towards a broken leader could be the steppingstone needed for repentance, revival, and restoration.

We're not talking about the Ananias that lied or condemned. This Ananias healed and restored. That's the difference.

6

RESTORING YOURSELF THROUGH REPENTANCE

S o, you're ready to change the course of your life and ministry? Of course, this is one of the greatest decisions that you can make and should be welcomed with a great deal of excitement. And so should the thought of repentance. Yes! Leaders need to repent too.

When Jesus begins his public ministry, we see that one of the first declarations he makes is, "Repent for the Kingdom of Heaven is at hand!" This was a bold proclamation not just to the regular layperson but also to every person in authority. Often, when leading and being the example to the flock of God, we miss out on the power that comes when we genuinely repent. Now, much of this repentance isn't before the congregations, although sometimes it will require that. This type of repentance goes into the heart of a leader and expresses the heartfelt desire for change and transformation.

Leaders, we can be doing a particular thing for so long that we forget the lasting implications that it has on our soul, ministry, and lives of those we lead. Sometimes, you've just got to want to be better for yourself. It doesn't mean that you're not concerned about your church or ministry, but you realize that you are more than what you have allowed or than you have demonstrated before God and man. I want you to hear that loudly. You are more.

There are times that repentance is initiated by brokenness, weeping, and travail. However, one of the most empowering experiences is to open your arms to redirection with joy and expectation. I wonder why no one taught us how to rejoice as we repent? Or how to dance as we asked for forgiveness? Subconsciously I think we have trained ourselves to avoid it like the plague as something to be avoided and not embraced.

When undergoing restoration as a leader, repentance must not be something that you shy away from. It also can't be something that you simply use as a method to say, "See, I've done it." As I have spoken to many leaders and experienced it myself, repentance has to be a deep action of the heart actually to change. Sometimes, leaders simply repent privately with no intention of doing things a different way. This form of repentance will only lead us back to the same brokenness, dysfunction, and unproductive habits. Repentance has to be a joy for you and not a feeling of sorrow. What's the use in looking good before man, wearing your fine apparel, and being spotlighted as being one of the kingdom's most remarkable gifts but look poorly in the eyes of God.

Wait! Isn't that the person that we want to please ultimately? Don't we want to do the things that honor Him the most? Too often, we are so inundated with the cares, responsibilities, and duties of ministry that we forget about the maintenance that must happen daily in our souls. I know that many of you are saying, "Well, I'm not sinning." I'm not saying that you are. You must understand that repentance isn't just about acknowledging what you have done. It is about recognizing your daily need for God and your desire to become all He has created you to be.

One of the things that we overcome daily through repentance is pride. It's hard to remain prideful when you have a consistent heart of repentance towards God. In addition to being repentant towards God, we must recognize our need to repent to others. This is an area that many leaders bypass on the road to becoming great. You can't misuse, hurt, damage, or cause God's people pain and be pleasing in His eyes. I know that some of you aren't aware of any hurt you have caused anyone, but the Holy Spirit does. I want you to take some time as you seek healing and restoration, to simply consider that you may have. This evaluation isn't to condemn yourself or make room for guilt or shame. It should be initiated with the hopes that the Holy Spirit will show you the situation.

Through humility, you now have an opportunity to make it right with that individual. There is so much power and grace you receive from God when you are willing to humble yourself and repent to people that might be in a lower status than you as a leader.

We all know that there are no statuses to God and that God loves all of us the same, but there are tiers in church government that can blind us from seeing one another that way. Wow! Isn't that something? When I am considering repenting to individuals as a leader, I must recognize that I must be willing to do the same to others if I am to expect others to repent to me. It doesn't matter who they are.

As you consider repenting, I want you to know that repentance does not blame others. When David confessed to God in Psalms 51, he made a point not to mention anyone else. There was no assignment of blame or responsibility on anyone but himself. The entire chapter is him taking responsibility for his actions and the consequences that he was experiencing. See, great leadership isn't just repenting but also accepting responsibility.

When walking the restorative process with individuals, the first thing I say to them is, "Take responsibility." It's easy to see the results of our actions and then use people as a bridge to why it occurred, but repentance cannot involve anyone else but yourself. It is then that God can work on the parts of your soul that opened the door to any area of failure or disappointment. You might not be able to control the character of others, but you are in control of yours and the doors you open to the enemy and his plan.

David accepted responsibility, but his son Saul did not. Instead, he blamed those around him. He implicated the troops and his need to please the people. He began to qualify is wrong decisions, and when you start justifying your choices as you repent, your repentance becomes impure.

In 1 Samuel 15:16-23, we witness the instructions of Samuel to Saul and, consequently, Saul's disobedience to carry it out. God had told Saul to destroy everything, but he keeps the livestock and the King alive to please the people. When he is confronted, he begins to shift the blame. Shifting blame when confronted by God as a leader is never a good thing. The only option is to repent.

See, God knows the details of the heart. There is nothing that you can hide from him. He knows what He said and also why you did what you did. Just repent.

When looking at these two examples, we see that David tells God that he would dare not bring a sacrifice as an atonement for his sin. Why? Because he knew that God wanted his heart. However, this was not the thinking of Saul. To appease God, Saul desired to make a sacrifice. He thought, "If I just give God this, it will be alright." You cannot bargain with God.

"The sacrifice pleasing to God is a broken spirit. You will not despise a broken and humbled heart, God." **Psalms 51:17**

Repentance is often thought of as something that we do as a recourse to failure instead of the key to experiencing total renewal and refreshing. While this is most certainly a spiritual act, it is also a conscious determination of the mind to become more productive executing God's original intent for your life. Many individuals will never experience this level of restoration. They have completed the spiritual aspect of this by asking for forgiveness but have never actually completed the last step. What is the last step? The last step to life restoration is communicating to **YOURSELF**. When was the last time that you had a conversation with yourself concerning your life's position? It's incredible how we can talk for countless hours to others but fail in our ability to confront and come to peace with ourselves. The peace that I'm speaking of is certainly not becoming "ok" with bad decisions, but you find rest in knowing that you still have an option. That option is to arise from the ashes of your situation and **RETURN** to the place where it all began.

What do you think would happen if you simply sat with yourself and came to peace with your past decisions, whether good or unfortunate? Are you still afraid to tell yourself that things have gotten a little ugly and just maybe you're the blame?

Refusing to accept responsibility will ultimately be the "sinful act" that causes many of us not to receive the promised place already provided.

"Who shall separate us from the love of Christ? Shall tribulation, or distress, or persecution or famine, or nakedness, or peril, or sword?" **Romans 8:35**

Isn't it amazing that Paul names things but calls them "Who's"? Situations can sometimes take on the persona of actual living beings that walk with you and even speak to you. And silencing them is, most of the time, one of the greatest battles. Many of you are reading this and witnessing that even though your world is not filled with many people, it is filled with many SITUATIONS. And not dealing with them will block those who are genuinely beneficial from reaching you. How many people have you blocked out of your life while keeping a relationship with an unresolved situation?

Honestly speaking, all of us, at some point, have had to come to the acknowledgment that we have moved outside of the original plan of God for our life because of a simple situation, whether it was emotional, physical, or mental. These transitions are often not intentional but are sometimes because of our inability to see clearly through it at any given time.

WHAT DID I WAKE UP TO?

What did you see more clearly the last time you woke up? Scripture shares with us concerning Samson and the terrible pickle he found himself in after a deep sleep on the wrong lap. Do you actually think that Samson didn't love God or didn't appreciate the power that was flowing through him? It was probably more about the need to escape a world that seemed as though he was isolated in. Have you ever found yourself outside of the original plan for your life, just trying to be normal?

Many of us have found ourselves in this exact situation. Attempting to maintain the history of our success while finding ourselves trying to escape its fame at the same time. Samson awakes and realizes that the direction he allowed himself to walk had caused him a great loss. This is where repentance heals.

DEALING WITH THE FACTS

Okay, the fact is that your decisions have caused inevitable consequences. The truth is that you are now awake and are looking at what you loved and realizing that it destroyed what was there. But the fact is also that much of what has been torn down in your life was never a permanent fixture in your future. No matter how much we think we know, God always knows and understands more. The absolute wisdom of God has made contingencies in the course of nature, and the universe is awaiting your awakening to help you get back on course.

"And he brought him forth abroad, and said, Look now toward heaven and tell the stars, if thou be able to number them: and he said unto him, So shall thy seed be. And he believed the Lord; and he counted it to him for righteousness." **Genesis 15:5**

Here in scripture, God instructs Abraham to look up to view the stars. One of the things that I don't believe we understand enough is that stars are beyond the earth realm. They have nothing to do with the earth or what's in it. Too often, we are concerned about what has happened or occurred in our lives that we forget that our view is to be towards those things that are ABOVE US.

If Abraham were ever to get off course, true repentance would be found simply by looking up. What is the permanent word of God for your life? What did He say? What did he promise?

This is genuine repentance, beloved. It is remembering the Word of God and returning to its power to bring you back.

Peter had done a terrible job at remaining consistent with his dedication to the Lord. But the Bible says that once everything had gone crazy...." HE REMEMBERED THE WORD OF THE LORD." As he remembers, the process of restoration begins.

What about the son who left his father's house and misspent his inheritance? He found himself in the hog's pen, but one day REMEMBERS. Is it possible that true repentance is in our remembrance of God's original plan for us and in our determination to get back to it?

REALIZING IT'S ALL GONE! STARTING OVER!

What is remarkable about repentance is that it starts the growing process all over again. Samson is imprisoned and blind but starts to regain his strength and power. Finding yourself at ground zero is sometimes the best place for you to be. Loss can be gain.

There will always be people who will look at the rubble and mourn your death. But rest assured that the ability of God to rebuild through repentance will astonish even the greatest of skeptics.

It is my prayer today that you have experienced the desire to remember and repent. Wake up tomorrow with a fresh look at your life and a more extraordinary view of the awesome plan for your future. Renewal and Restoration have come. Be the Ananias that you are to other people! Heal thyself!

CALL ME ANANIAS

7

KEYS TO RESTORATION

I don't think that I have said this during our time together, but I think it's time as we prepare to conclude. The restoration process is not easy. There will be moments where you want to give up and when you think that it's not worth it at all. However, I want you to know that it is. What has happened in your heart as you have read this book is more monumental than you can ever imagine. There is a new spark of power being ignited within you, and God will use that to blaze something powerful.

The word restore means to simply give something back or return to someone something that was lost or stolen. It means to return something to its original condition through repair or cleaning. When we think about our lives and all of the nasty, hurtful, and disappointing experiences, we can all attest that we need to be restored. Many of us have served God with all of our hearts and always strived to do what's right, but have gotten scared and stained in the process.

It's a powerful thought to embrace when thinking about the great potential that you still have to change the world. Sometimes, we are looking at where we've come and how far we still have to go. The thought can become heavy, and we can become weary with even the idea of having to put more work in to get to the place we desire in our hearts. This is not an isolated experience. Many of God's greatest vessels are right there with you.

However, I want to show you a few things about restoration and how God pushes you to see yourself as something greater. I know that we have an idea of how great we are, but have you ever considered that it is only a small percentage of your potential through Christ. Let's take a look at what the Bible says in Revelations 2:4-5.

"Nevertheless, I have somewhat against thee, because thou hast left thy first love. Remember therefore from whence thou art fallen, and repent, and do the first works; or else I will come unto thee quickly and will remove thy candlestick out of his place, except thou repent."

The first thing that is noted here is the decrease of love. Whenever our love and passion for God decreases, we are more open to things or people who will not encourage us to continue leading and being the example that He has called us to be. Some of you have not stopped leading, but you are not doing it as passionately as you have before because of certain situations. You still love God, but you do not like His church or people as much as you once did. You need to be restored.

When we look in Luke 15:8-9, we see a powerful illustration of a woman still living in her house, but something most valuable had been lost. It's possible to continue leading and be without the internal resources needed to continue doing it in joy. This entire book has been about our need for restoration. Unfortunately, many of us never knew that we were broken. Hopefully, after reading, you see areas that need to be mended. Any area within us that is disconnected is without power and the creative ability to move forward through where you are now and into the future God has planned.

"Either what woman having ten pieces of silver, if she lose one piece, doth light a candle, and sweep the house, and seek diligently till she find it? And when she hath found it, she calleth her friends and her neighbors together, saying, Rejoice with me; for I have found the piece which I had lost."

One of the first things that this woman in scripture does is recognize what's missing. I want you to think about any area of your life that is missing an essential element. Are you still leading as vibrantly as you did before? Are you missing the passion you once had? Are you still looking for the support needed to fulfill God's assignment for your life or ministry?

Often, after our life's battles and our journey in ministry, there are parts of us that have disappeared. Unfortunately, many of us don't recognize it. The people around us do. As an exercise, I want you to consider having a conversation with some of your closest disciples.

I want you to ask them about any area you were once strong in but now are not. Immediately, when some of you read that, you said to yourself, "No, I can't do that." My question is, why not?

Sometimes, our pride will cause us not to see what's disappeared, areas that we have forgotten about, or vital elements that God always intended us to use. You must remember that those closest to us can see the areas of our ministries that have weakened.

In addition to this, we can also mourn the results of occurrences that were our victories. Do you remember David and how Saul threatened his life over and over again? Once David received word that Saul was dead and the threat was extinguished, he began to mourn terribly. Until one day, Joab rebukes him about it (2 Samuel 19). David had thrown himself into such a period of mourning that it was causing the people who were fighting with him to lose their morale. What looked like a win didn't feel like a win to him.

As leaders, we can have this same experience. We can come through some of the greatest battles in ministry and mourn the loss of people who were simply casualties of war. Friends, I want you to release yourself from any guilt and shame you still carry because of who you lost during the process. Sometimes, we are still grieving people who left right or who left wrongly. In doing this, we are taking away honor from those who are left behind.

The people watched David mourn. Did he have a right to grieve? Yes! The friend who he loved was now dead. The man who he ministered to as King was now dead as well. This was not the way David wanted things to turn out.

There will always be circumstances that we would've hoped turn out a different way but didn't. However, it will be up to you what happens next. Will you continue mourning and weeping over what's unrecoverable, or will you find out what you can salvage and restore.

The woman in Luke 15 does some things that I want to take a moment to point out. Firstly, she recognizes what's missing. One of the best ways to recognize what's missing is to remember what it looked like before. How did you leave it? If you are a leader, I want you to begin to pull out those old cassettes. I know that many of you still have them. Find those classic sermons of your youth and listen to them. Listen for the enthusiasm and strength in your voice. These exercises are not to get you in a mood of longing for your old glory days but to cause you to recognize that you are the same vessel today. I know that you might be weary from the battle, but isn't God the same God that renews your strength like the eagles.

You're not that immature person anymore. You have the wisdom of the ages with you now and the experience needed to be more strategic in how you execute the Lord's plan for your life and ministry. If God allowed anything to occur in your life, it is with an intention that you use it for His glory.

An example of recognizing what's missing is found in 1 Samuel 30:3-4. David and his men came back to the city and discovered that the city was burned with fire. They also notice that their wives, sons, and daughters were taken captive as well. Wow! Doesn't the enemy know how to target the heart of God's leaders? One of the areas that I want you to receive healing in is the loss of people. Many of you started with those that you assumed would be with you forever, but they've departed. I want you to accept that some people are gone forever, but others are just gone for a moment. It's not your job to run after them in a way that lowers your integrity or value for yourself.

Nevertheless, if you don't begin the healing process, if God decides to send some back to you, you won't be healed enough to receive them in joy and through the heart of Christ. David notices that those closest to his heart were gone. He and his men lifted their voices and wept.

When is the last time that you wept over what's missing? When is the last time you allowed yourself to experience the emotions in your heart that are human? Yes, I know that you are supernaturally infused, but God needs your vulnerability in every area. He needs you to express what you have felt, so that He can provide you with the grace to stand and still expect His goodness. They lifted their voices and wept. However, the story does not end with their weeping. Aren't we glad about that? They wept, but David also prayed.

Can I ask you a question, "What are you going to do after you finish weeping?" These men wept until they had no more power to weep, but after they finished, the Bible says, David inquired of the Lord.

"And David enquired at the Lord, saying, Shall I pursue after this troop? Shall I overtake them? And he answered him, Pursue: for thou shalt surely overtake them and without fail recover all."

1 Samuel 30:8

There must now be a point in your life and ministry that you get up from weeping. I know that it's not been as easy as you imagined and much more challenging than you expected, but God still has a plan. God begins to give David instructions on what to do and how to recover what he lost. God tells him how to be restored. Being obedient to God's plan, David recovers all and increases well beyond what he originally had.

Here are a few points that I believe will lead you into recovery and restoration:

Bring light to dark places: The enemy loves to use the hidden places in our lives to hide what we need the most. He'll allow you to live in the dens, caves, and strongholds

CALL ME ANANIAS

we spoke of earlier to stop us from discovering that we still have the power to move out of them. In this season of your life, the Word of God must be the light that shines in that dark place.

"Thy word is a lamp unto my feet and a light unto my path."
Psalms 119:105

Remember where you lost it: Often, it's not that we don't have the strength to recover and be restored. We just don't know where we have lost it. Listen, if we can be honest, some of us have flat-out lost it. We may not have lost physically, but mentally, spiritually, and emotionally some things are gone. I want you to increase your time in prayer. Allow God to take you back to places in your experience that took away the tools that you were using to build.

In 2 Kings 6:5, one of the sons of the prophets had a zeal to help build a larger place for them to dwell. Because he didn't own one himself, he goes to borrow one from a neighbor. In the process of his building, the ax head falls in the water. He loses what he was using to build, and he is now having to deal with the consequences of losing

Page 148

something that didn't belong to him. He goes to the man of God and tells him what just happened. The Prophet of God asks him something powerful, "Where did it fall?" See, one of the keys to restoration will always be locating the area that you fell or that something did. If you can pinpoint it through the Spirit's power, you can regain the tool you need to continue advancing the plan of God. God has an extraordinary way of bringing things back to the surface, even when we think we've lost them for good.

Do what it takes to get whole: Your restoration is all that matters. You shouldn't take unnecessary time attempting to please everyone. Sometimes, we hinder our restoration process by thinking about how others feel about the necessary steps for our healing. When we look at 2 Kings 5:1, we see the story of Naaman. Naaman was a captain of the host of the King of Syria and was a great and honorable man. Through him, the Bible says the Lord had given them great deliverance. He was a mighty man of valor but was also a leper. Leprosy was one of the most despised diseases in scripture.

Interestingly, his name meant to be delightful, pleasant, and beautiful, but the image he was displaying was the exact opposite. He had position, popularity, and prestige, but now all of that was marred because of his brokenness and disease.

So, Naaman decides to come to the door of the Prophet Elisha to receive healing. He comes in haughty and prideful. Remember, we talked about pride earlier *(1 Peter 5:5)*. The Prophet Elisha sends word for him to wash in a dirty river and that his flesh would come back as a newborn baby. Instead of him giving glory to God at the opportunity to be restored, he begins to complain at the method chosen to bring him healing.

Sometimes, God can give us a clear path forward and a way to come back into power, but we aren't willing to do what it takes to get there. Pride will stop the process of your restoration every time. I want you to understand something. Some of God's greatest deliverances are done with small instructions. Don't allow your pride to hinder the healing and restoration you know you need.

Friends, there are steps that the Lord will give you after reading this book. There will be moments where you will be glad to do them and then points along the way where your flesh will try to resist. Don't fight back. I want you to yield to the Lord's strategies because His ultimate goal is your restoration and His ability to use you to restore others. Keep going, Ananias. Your restoration is coming!

8

BROTHER SAUL

" And Ananias went his way and entered into the house; and putting his hands on him said, Brother Saul, the Lord, even Jesus, that appeared unto thee in the way as thou camest, hath sent me, that thou mightest receive thy sight, and be filled with the Holy Ghost. So Ananias departed and entered the house. And laying his hands on him, he said, "Brother Saul, the Lord Jesus who appeared to you on the road by which you came has sent me so that you may regain your sight and be filled with the Holy Spirit. And immediately there fell from his eyes as it had been scales: and he received sight forthwith, and arose, and was baptized. And immediately, something like scales fell from his eyes, and he regained his sight. Then he rose and was baptized. And when he had received meat, he was strengthened. Then was Saul certain days with the disciples which were at Damascus, and taking food, he was strengthened. For some days he was with the disciples at Damascus. And straightway he preached Christ in the

synagogues, that he is the Son of God."
Acts 9:17-20

After receiving God's instruction to go to Saul, Ananias submits to God's plan and goes as he was commanded. As he enters the house, he immediately puts his hands on him and calls him something many of us would not have. He says, "Brother Saul."

I wanted to end by showing you a few powerful things from the conclusion of this very compelling story. I want to begin by showing you how sons restore the confidence of fathers. Saul was certainly not raised in the house of Ananias to be considered his son. Still, the impartation through Ananias' hands would be the first physical expression of the touch of Christ he experienced. As much as Saul needed Ananias, Ananias needed Saul.

Suppose you understood the secrecy and hiding Ananias was probably accustomed to. In that case, you can imagine the fear that might've gripped him to do anything publicly, especially to someone who had threatened them with so much vigor. Even though he was fearful, he went to embrace someone who once was an enemy.

Friends, there's a level of confidence that God is about to restore to you because of your ability to remain touchable to those coming to you. Sometimes, when we have experienced betrayal, our hearts can become hardened. We now just want to minister to those we have known and shut ourselves away from anyone new. Ananias was most likely accustomed to worshipping and teaching those who he knew he was safe around. However, God was opening up his heart in a way that would show him that he still had more to offer.

If you are a leader reading this, you have probably touched thousands of lives throughout your ministry. Some of them come back to say thank you, while many have continued on their way without ever recognizing that you were the bridge that helped them get over. I don't want you to allow that to stop you. God is about to send you to a new generation of people that might've not known him before. He's also about to send you to people who the kingdom has known, but because of certain events they've been discarded.

There's something powerful that grows in our hearts when we allow God to develop us behind the scenes. See, being a public gift is good, but it can sometimes take away from the private experiences we need with God. Those personal experiences thrust us into power with God and the ability to touch even the lowest among us.

God chose Ananias for a reason. God saw that the heart of Ananias wasn't contaminated by the need to be famous or great. Ananias served God faithfully without the glamor of what we see today as a success. His success was found in his passion for God and his love for God's people.

As you have read this book, I pray that your desire to be used by God has increased. I pray that you are now willing to open your heart to be healed and be used as a healer to the broken, forgotten, and lost. You have what it takes, Ananias. Go! God is with you.

There's something that I want to point out to you about the way Ananias approached Saul. He didn't come to him with lies, as the first Ananias. He didn't approach him with judgment and cruelty as Ananias, the High Priest, would later treat him. He came to him humbly honoring his assignment to heal. Often, many of God's broken leaders aren't recovered because of how the wrong ones have approached them. He goes into the house and immediately lays his hands on his eyes. He calls him brother!

He says, *"Brother Saul, the Lord Jesus who appeared to you on the road by which you came has sent me so that you may regain your sight and be filled with the Holy Spirit."*

If you would stop and just listen to the powerful intent behind those words, you would see the need for us to express that same heart to others. It's one thing to call someone a friend, colleague, or buddy. However, it's something else to call them, Brother. Whenever a person is entitled to any familial status, it shows a greater responsibility and attachment to that person.

When walking individuals through the restorative process, it's essential to see them as you see yourself. Ananias wasn't just saying that Saul was someone that he would merely lay hands on. He was seeing him as himself. How?

He knew that the same Jesus that Saul needed was the same one that he did too.

Often, individuals aren't healed through our lives because we are not seeing them as we do ourselves. One of the things that Jesus taught us is to treat others the same way we desire to be treated. This means that if we see a brother or a sister in any situation of brokenness that we are immediately to consider ourselves.

Considering ourselves doesn't mean to hope that we are never broken like they are. It means to visualize yourself as that person. What would happen if every time you saw a sick person, you saw yourself? Wouldn't that make you pray for them with more vigor? What if when you saw that falling leader, you pictured yourself? Would that make you restore and heal with more compassion?

See, for you to be an Ananias to this generation, you will have to lower the way you see yourself and place yourself on the same level as someone else. We are all in need of God. We are all in need of His love and compassion.

Suddenly, the Bible says that the scales fall from the eyes of Saul, and he was filled with the Holy Spirit. What a sudden transformation and an example of the results of one man's obedience. If God would've asked anyone else, they might not have gone, or they might've gone with a different plan.

God knows who to put in the hands of certain people. And what I am prophetically declaring to you is that God is about to put some of his most chosen vessels in your hands. I know that some of you are saying, "Well, I'm the one that needs to be restored." I get that, but I want you to remember what Jesus told Peter in Luke 22:31-32. Jesus had just confronted Peter concerning the enemy's plan to sift him as wheat. The devil wanted the future of Peter and ultimately the lives of everyone that Peter would later touch.

Leaders, the enemy planned to get you so discouraged that you would lose sight of the future and the generations you were designed to impact. But he is a liar! You will be restored and healed and will, as a result, heal and restore others.

Jesus tells Peter, *"But I have prayed for thee, that thy faith fail not: and when thou art converted, strengthen thy brethren."*

I know that you have suffered a lot and have experienced many things, but there's still a demand for your assignment on the earth. God is saying to you that, *"I'm going to restore you and after I do, go heal others."* You might need an Ananias, but today I want you to realize that you are an Ananias too! Go and Heal!

Made in the USA
Middletown, DE
27 July 2023

35820419R00099